JN065998

Elevate your English
with
Shadowing
—VOA Learning English

Atsuko Kuramoto / Harumi Nishida / Chie Tsurii / John Nevara

SANSHUSHA

音声ダウンロード＆ストリーミングサービス(無料)のご案内

https://www.sanshusha.co.jp/text/onsei/isbn/9784384335316/

本書の音声が、上記アドレスよりダウンロードおよびストリーミング再生できます。ぜひご利用ください。

＊本書では１つの記事につき、**Slow スピードと Natural スピードの２種類の音声**を用意
しています。どちらも米国発音のネイティブスピーカーによる朗読です。Slow スピード
のものは VOA Learning English のオリジナル音声となっております。

Photos

は じ め に

　21世紀に入り四半期を迎える今、自然環境、紛争、ジェンダーなど数えきれない国際問題を抱えるなか、人々の生活に大きな影響を与えるAIが占める役割が格段に増しています。AIがいともたやすく翻訳結果を出す状況となってきました。しかしその翻訳結果をそのまますべて受け入れて良いかどうかは慎重でなければなりません。

　このような状況下では、日本語での読解力に加え、英語による情報の読解力も身につけておくことは有益でしょう。その際、記述されていることがらを正確に読み解くことが必要になります。また、AIから産出される言語表現についても適切であるかを判断するスキルがこれまで以上に大切になります。

　揺れ動く世界情勢のなかで事実関係を的確にとらえることのできる読み解く力を身につけるには、まず語彙や文法の知識を持っていなければなりません。しかしこれらの知識が自然に身につくほど日常の生活場面で英語に接する機会はありません。

　日本語の文章を理解するときには、読み取った文字を頭の中で音声化して理解するという処理を無意識に行っています。外国語である英語文を読むときにも同様の処理をしますので、リーディング力を伸ばすにはリスニング力を支える「音声知覚力」を鍛えなければなりません。

　「音声知覚力」とは言語の処理能力のひとつで、発話されている語やひとかたまりの語句の音声を即座に知覚することができる能力のことを指します。この「音声知覚力」を短期間で効果的に伸長させる方法として、シャドーイング練習を繰り返すことが提唱されています。シャドーイング練習により伸びた「音声知覚力」は、音声と文字の関係をより速く結びつける補助となり、記述された文章のリーディング力を伸長させることにつながるのです。

　本書では半期または通年の授業中、毎回30分以内の取り組みで効果の現れる適量として、各ユニットの始めに約100語のシャドーイング用素材を用意しました。

　さらに皆さんが興味を持って聞き、読み進むことができるよう、今を映し出す新鮮なニュース記事を取り上げています。私たちが住む地球環境を守ることを目指したSustainable Development Goals (SDGs) の話題を中心に、企業や国際機関、個人、研究者、アーティストら、さまざまな人々の努力や取り組みを伝えています。無理なくより高度な運用力を養えるようにシャドーイング練習の4つのステップを示し、その復習を促す構成にしました。

　皆さんが本書のシャドーイング練習を通して「音声知覚力」を高め、その結果としてリーディングの速さや正確さを増し、英語運用力を伸ばすことを願ってやみません。

編著者

Table of Contents

シャドーイング（Shadowing）練習法とは

概　要

　シャドーイングとは、聞こえてくる英語音声を追いかけて、そのモデル音声とほぼ同時に発話する、"影"のように声を出して練習する方法のことです。英語の特徴的な音声に対する理解を深め、英語のリズム感をつかみ、ナチュラルスピードで話すトレーニングにもなり、結果として文意もつかめるようになります。この練習法は、通訳の卵たちがその養成機関において頻繁に実施している練習法で、効果の程はその後の彼らの通訳業務で発揮する実力からも間違いないものといえます。

　VOA（Voice of America）Learning English の authentic English（生きている現場の英語）は、世界で起こる出来事について毎日インターネット上で配信されている英語放送です。VOA Learning English は、英語を学んでいる人のために基本使用語彙数を1,500語程度に絞り、通常の英語ニュースより3割程度遅いスピードでの放送となっています。本書では、VOA Learning English のオリジナル音声に加え、アメリカ英語の母語話者によるナチュラルスピードでの吹き替え版2種の音声を収録し、異なるスピードでの練習ができるようにしました。

　下に示す具体的なシャドーイング手順や注意点は、テキストの要所に示しています。また、\\ Let's Try Shadowing! // 部分を授業で初めて実施したときに、毎回自己評価して Great! / Good! / Not too bad! / Tough! という4段階の記録を残し、次の段階に進む励みにするための表を設けています。

　\\ Let's Try Shadowing! // は **STEP 1** から **STEP 4** の段階を追った発話練習を行い、続いて、ニュースの内容をパラフレーズする問題やニュースに出てきた語彙を異なる文脈で使う問題などを行った後に、Let's Talk で記事内容にかかわる自由な話し合いができるような課題を用意しました。

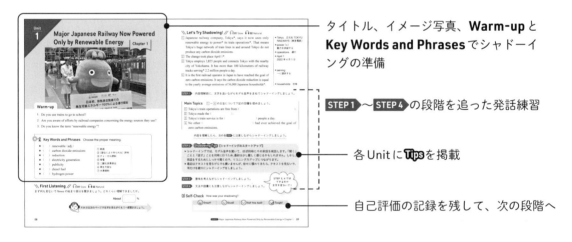

タイトル、イメージ写真、**Warm-up** と **Key Words and Phrases** でシャドーイングの準備

STEP 1 ～ **STEP 4** の段階を追った発話練習

各 Unit に **Tips** を掲載

自己評価の記録を残して、次の段階へ

\\ Let's Try Shadowing! // での具体的なシャドーイング手順

① **シャドーイングする準備**：各 Unit のタイトルを読み、イメージ写真を見た後に、**Warm-up** の質問に回答しながら、記事に書かれていると予測できる分野について知っている知識を活性化させる。**Key Words and Phrases** で当該 Unit を理解するうえで重要な語句を押さえておく。

② **STEP 1** 内容理解をする前に、文字を追いながらモデル音声をまねてシャドーイングする。この段階では、すべての語を追いかけられなくても気にせず、次に聞こえてくる語を発話しよう。

③ STEP2 各Unitの< **Main Topics** >で記事の前半の内容をparaphrase（言い換え）し、理解したうえで、STEP2 に記載しているコツ **Shadowing Tips** を参照してシャドーイングする。Unitが進むごとにシャドーイングするときの異なる特徴を提示しているので、それらのコツを積み重ねて習得していく。

④ STEP3 慣れてきたら音声を追うだけではなく、意味を考えながらシャドーイングする。

⑤ STEP4 仕上げに、< **Main Topics** >で理解した内容に基づいて、文法や語彙にも注意しながらシャドーイングする。

⑥ ＼＼ **Let's Try Shadowing Again!** ／／ のところでNewsの始まり部分または全体をもう一度練習しよう。この時にしっかり意味・文法・語彙にも注意を向けられるようにしよう。

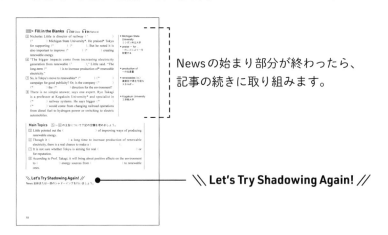

Newsの始まり部分が終わったら、記事の続きに取り組みます。

＼＼ **Let's Try Shadowing Again!** ／／

Tips 1　初めて聞く時からすべての内容を無理やり理解しようとせず、まず、音声をまねて追うことから始めましょう。途中の段階（ STEP1 ）で内容の要点をとらえるため一度paraphraseします。

Tips 2　その後、STEP2 から STEP4 へと回数を重ね練習を続けることで、聞こえてきた音声をまねるだけでなく、聞くと同時に意味を部分的に汲み取るところから全容を汲み取るスキルをつけ、リスニング力を高めることができるでしょう。

Tips 3　「はじめに」にも書きましたが、私たちは文章を理解するときに、自分では気づかないまま文字を音声化して意味を理解するという処理を行っています。外国語である英語文を読むときにも同様の処理をしますので、シャドーイング回数を重ねることが文章理解の助けとなっていきます。

レベルに応じた練習手順の例

初級・中級レベル　例　文字提示ありのシャドーイング
　　　　　　　　　　　① 文字を見ながら、音声を追いかけて発話練習する。（2回）
　　　　　　　　　　　② 文字を隠して、音声を追いかけて発話練習する。（1回）

中級・上級レベル　例　文字提示なしのシャドーイング
　　　　　　　　　　　① 文字を隠して、音声を追いかけて発話練習する。（1回目：わかる語のみ追いかける、2回目：音声に注意しながら、3回目：意味を考えながら）
　　　　　　　　　　　② ①の後で文字を確認する。

Major Japanese Railway Now Powered Only by Renewable Energy

Chapter 1

Warm-up

1. Do you use trains to go to school?

2. Are you aware of efforts by railroad companies concerning the energy sources they use?

3. Do you know the term "renewable energy"?

🔑 Key Words and Phrases   Choose the proper meaning.

- (　) renewable（adj.）
- (　) carbon dioxide emissions
- (　) reduction
- (　) electricity generation
- (　) publicity
- (　) diesel fuel
- (　) hydrogen power

① 削減
② (宣伝により作られる) 評判
③ ディーゼル燃料
④ 発電
⑤ 二酸化炭素排出
⑥ 再生可能な
⑦ 水素燃料

\\ First Listening // 🎧 01 Slow 🎧 02 Natural

まず何も見ないで News の始まり部分を聞きましょう。どれくらい理解できましたか。

About 　　　 %

それでは次のページで文字を見ながらもう一度聞きましょう。 ➡

\\ **Let's Try Shadowing!** // 🎧 **01** Slow 🎧 **02** Natural

1. Japanese railway company, Tokyu*, says it now uses only renewable energy to power* its train operations*. That means Tokyu's huge network of train lines in and around Tokyo do not produce any carbon dioxide emissions.
2. The change took place April 1*.
3. Tokyu employs 3,855 people and connects Tokyo with the nearby city of Yokohama. It has more than 100 kilometers of railway tracks serving* 2.2 million people a day.
4. It is the first railroad operator in Japan to have reached the goal of zero carbon emissions. It says the carbon dioxide reduction is equal to the yearly average emissions of 56,000 Japanese households*.

* Tokyu　正式名 TOKYU RAILWAYS（東急電鉄）
* power (v.) 動力を供給する
* operations　運行
* April 1 2022 年 4 月 1 日
* serving 〜に提供する
* households　世帯

STEP 1 ▶ 内容理解前に、文字を追いながらモデル音声をまねてシャドーイングしましょう。

Main Topics   1〜4 の主旨について下記の空欄を埋めましょう。

1. Tokyu's train operations are free from (   ).
2. Tokyu made the (   ).
3. Tokyu's train service is for (   ) people a day.
4. No other (   ) had ever achieved the goal of zero carbon emissions.

内容を理解したら、次の各 **STEP** ▶ に注意しながらシャドーイングしましょう。

STEP 2 ▶ **Shadowing Tips**【シャドーイングのスタートアップ】

▶ シャドーイングでは、モデル音声を聞いて、ほぼ同時にその英語を発話します。「聞く」ことと「話す」ことを同時に行うため、最初は少し難しく感じるかもしれません。しかし、発話をするためにしっかり聞くので、リスニング力アップにつながります。

▶ 最初はテキストを見ながらでも構いませんが、徐々に慣れてきたら、テキストを見ないで、耳だけを頼りにシャドーイングをしましょう。

STEP 3 ▶ 意味を考えながらシャドーイングしましょう。

STEP 4 ▶ 文法や語彙にも注意しながらシャドーイングしましょう。

> STEP 3, 4 では できるだけ 文字を見ないで！

☑ **Self-Check**   How was your shadowing?

😄 Great!	🙂 Good!	😐 Not too bad!	😣 Tough!

5 Nicholas Little is director of railway (¹   )
(²   ) Michigan State University*. He praised* Tokyu
for supporting (³   ) (⁴   ). But he noted it is
also important to improve (⁵   ) (⁶   ) creating
renewable energy.

6 "The bigger impacts come from increasing electricity
generation from renewable (⁷   )," Little said. "The
long-term (⁸   ) is to increase production of* renewable
electricity."

7 So, is Tokyu's move to renewables* (⁹   ) (¹⁰   )
campaign for good publicity? Or, is the company (¹¹   )
(¹²   ) the (¹³   ) direction for the environment?

8 There is no simple answer, says one expert. Ryo Takagi
is a professor at Kogakuin University* and specialist in
(¹⁴   ) railway systems. He says bigger (¹⁵   )
(¹⁶   ) would come from changing railroad operations
from diesel fuel to hydrogen power or switching to electric
automobiles.

* Michigan State
University
ミシガン州立大学

* praise ～ for ...
...のことにより～を
称賛する

* production of
～の生産量

* renewables (n.)
複数形で再生可能な
エネルギー

* Kogakuin University
工学院大学

Main Topics   5 ～ 8 の主旨について下記の空欄を埋めましょう。

5 Little pointed out the (   ) of improving ways of producing
renewable energy.

6 Though it (   ) a long time to increase production of renewable
electricity, there is a real chance to make a (   ).

7 It is not sure whether Tokyu is aiming for real (   ) or
for reputation.

8 According to Prof. Takagi, it will bring about positive effects on the environment
to (   ) energy sources from (   ) to renewable
ones.

\\ Let's Try Shadowing Again! //

News 全体または一部のシャドーイングを行いましょう。

➡️ Comprehension

A Fill in the blanks.

Statistics and Actions by Tokyu and Other Experts		
Tokyu	The number of employees	(1.)
	The number of daily passengers	(2.)
	The length of its railway tracks	(3.)
	Its CO_2 reduction	Equal to the yearly average emissions of (4.) Japanese (5.)
	Adopted	(6.) to power its train operations
	Made the change in its railroad operations	on (7.)
Nicholas Little	His note	The importance of improving how to (8.) renewable energy
Ryo Takagi	His recommendation	To change energy (9.) from traditional ones to renewable ones

B Vocabulary: Choose the appropriate word. Change the form if necessary.

1. Recent posts on social media have (   ) people's feeling.
2. One beer can (   ) your driving.
3. Could you please (   ) your seat with mine?
4. Wine will be (   ) at the party.
5. The company plans (   ) a larger volume of its core product than before.

switch / produce / fuel / impact / serve

Summary of the News Choose the appropriate word.

Tokyu (1.   ) the goal of zero carbon emissions for the first time among railroad (2.   ) in Japan. A director of railway education in Michigan praised its (3.   ). But he noted the importance of (4.   ) efforts to increase production of renewable electricity. Professor Takagi also (5.   ) the necessity of (6.   ) energy sources.

keeping / switching / achievement / operators / achieved / indicates

Let's Talk ── Talk about the changes that Tokyu has made to its train operations to reduce carbon emissions.

Major Japanese Railway Now Powered Only by Renewable Energy

Chapter 2

Warm-up

1. What are some traditional energy sources?

2. What are some renewable energies?

3. Do you know the meaning of the word "geothermal"?

🔑 Key Words and Phrases   Choose the proper meaning.

- ( ) critical
- ( ) polluter
- ( ) behind (adv.)
- ( ) hydropower
- ( ) geothermal-power
- ( ) utility
- ( ) nuclear disaster
- ( ) coal-fired power plants

① 水力発電
② 地熱発電
③ 石炭火力発電所
④ 極めて重要な
⑤ 公害を引き起こす組織
⑥ 原子力災害
⑦ 遅れて
⑧ 公益事業体（電気・ガス・水道など）

⟍ First Listening ⫽   🎧 05 Slow   🎧 06 Natural

まず何も見ないで News の始まり部分を聞きましょう。
どれくらい理解できましたか。

About [   ] %

それでは次のページで文字を見ながらもう一度聞きましょう。 ➡

\\ Let's Try Shadowing! // 🎧 05 Slow 🎧 06 Natural

1. Tokyu's action is better than nothing*, but Takagi said, "I am not going out of my way to* praise it as great."
2. Tokyu official* Yoshimasa Kitano says the company plans more action toward cleaner operations.
3. "We don't see this as reaching our goal but just a start," Kitano said.
4. Such steps are critical for Japan, the world's sixth-biggest carbon polluter. The country has a goal of becoming carbon-neutral* by the year 2050.

* better than nothing 何もないよりましだ
* going out of my way to 〜するために（時間をかけて・わざわざ無理をして）尽力する
* official 職員
* carbon-neutral CO_2 の排出量と吸収量のバランスが取れ、実質 CO_2 ゼロ

STEP 1 内容理解前に、文字を追いながらモデル音声をまねてシャドーイングしましょう。

Main Topics ①〜④ の主旨について下記の空欄を埋めましょう。

1. Takagi won't waste his time making positive comments about (   ) action.
2. Kitano announces that Tokyu will further increase the (   ).
3. Kitano clearly said that Tokyu's present change is just a (   ) step.
4. Japan, the (   ) carbon polluter, sets a national goal to be (   ) by 2050.

内容を理解したら、次の各 **STEP** に注意しながらシャドーイングしましょう。

STEP 2 **Shadowing Tips** 【音の特徴】

▶ 日本語と英語には、リズム、イントネーション、音声変化などの音声上の違いがあります。どのようなリズム、イントネーションで発話されているのか、音はどのように変化しているのかに注意して聞きましょう。

▶ 英語のリズム、イントネーション、音声変化の特徴がわかると聞き取りやすくなります。さらに自分の発音も向上して一石二鳥です。

STEP 3 意味を考えながらシャドーイングしましょう。

STEP 4 文法や語彙にも注意しながらシャドーイングしましょう。

> STEP 3, 4 では
> できるだけ
> 文字を見ないで！

☑ Self-Check How was your shadowing?

😄 Great!	🙂 Good!	😐 Not too bad!	😥 Tough!

5 About 20 percent of Japan's (^{1}) (^{2}) (^{3}) renewable sources, says Japan's Institute for Sustainable Energy Policies*.

6 That is far behind New Zealand, for example, where (^{4}) (^{5}) of power used comes from renewable energy sources. New Zealand hopes to make that* 100 percent (^{6}) (^{7}).

7 The renewable sources driving Tokyu trains include hydropower, geothermal-power, wind power and solar power. That information comes from Tokyo Electric Power Co.*, the utility that provides the electricity and looks at (^{8}) (^{9}) (^{10}).

8 Since Japan's 2011 nuclear disaster in Fukushima, the country has (^{11}) (^{12}) most of its nuclear plants* and increased (^{13}) (^{14}) coal-fired power plants.

9 Japan aims to have 36 to 38 percent (^{15}) (^{16}) energy come from renewable sources by 2030.

* Institute for Sustainable Energy Policies 環境エネルギー政策研究所 (ISEP)

* that は下記の指示代名詞 "power used... sources"

* Tokyo Electric Power Co. 東京電力ホールディングス

* nuclear plants 原子力発電所

Main Topics   5 ～ 9 の主旨について下記の空欄を埋めましょう。

5 According to ISEP, approximately one (   ) of Japan's electricity comes from renewable sources.

6 (   ) achievement rate in switching to renewable energy sources is far behind (   ).

7 Tokyu adopts (   ) as their renewable sources.

8 Because of (   ) in Fukushima, Japan increased use of coal-fired power plants.

9 By 2030, Japan targets generation of (   ) of its energy from renewable sources.

\\ Let's Try Shadowing Again! //

News 全体または一部のシャドーイングを行いましょう。

➡ Comprehension

A Fill in the blanks.

Year	Country	Future Plan of Energy
(1.)	Japan	reaches (2.) of 36 to 38 percent of its energy from renewable sources.
(3.)	New Zealand	(4.) to realize using (5.) renewable energy resources.
2050	Japan	hopes to become (6.).

B Vocabulary: Choose the appropriate word. Change the form if necessary.

1. The financial situation in our company turned (   ) due to the slowing economy.
2. All the team members made efforts to (   ) their previous record.
3. That river has Lake Biwa as its (   ).
4. All citizens should be very careful not to (   ) the rivers.
5. All cars in the near future might be (   ) by electricity.

> power / source / pollute / critical / better

Summary of the News Choose the appropriate word(s).

A Tokyu official says the company will (1.   ) further action toward CO_2-free operations. Japan's (2.   ) on non-renewable energy sources is far (3.   ) compared to that of (4.   ). As of now, approximately (5.   ) of Japan's electricity comes from renewable sources. Besides that, its target value (6.   ) is quite low.

> higher / by 2030 / take / New Zealand / 20 percent / dependence

Let's Talk — Talk about why taking steps towards cleaner operations is critical for Japan.

Underwater Drone Measures Ocean Carbon Levels

Chapter 1

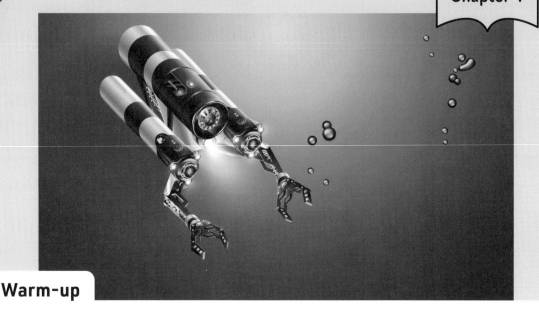

Warm-up

1. Have you ever seen a drone flying?

2. Did you know that some drones can dive into the ocean?

3. What are drones used for?

4. What are the causes of CO_2 emissions?

🔑 **Key Words and Phrases**   Choose the proper meaning.

- ( ) drone
- ( ) carbon dioxide (CO_2) levels
- ( ) glider
- ( ) climate change
- ( ) ocean's chemistry
- ( ) ocean acidification
- ( ) CO_2 emissions
- ( ) uptake

① 気候変動
② 取り込み
③ 二酸化炭素濃度
④ 二酸化炭素排出
⑤ ドローン
⑥ グライダー
⑦ 海洋酸性化
⑧ 海洋の化学的性質

＼ First Listening ／／ 🎧 09 Slow 🎧 10 Natural

まず何も見ないで News の始まり部分を聞きましょう。
どれくらい理解できましたか。

About 　　　　 %

それでは次のページで文字を見ながらもう一度聞きましょう。　➡

\\ Let's Try Shadowing! // 🎧09 Slow 🎧10 Natural

1. Researchers are using an underwater drone to measure carbon dioxide (CO_2) levels in the ocean. It is believed to be the first time such a vehicle* has been used specifically to test* CO_2 levels.

2. The vehicle, which the team also calls a glider, is designed to dive down to 1,000 meters in deep ocean areas and can operate for weeks at a time*.

3. The goal of the research is to provide scientists with data about how climate change is affecting the ocean's chemistry. The self-swimming drone was deployed* in the Gulf of Alaska* this spring. Reporters from The Associated Press* recently joined researchers on a boat in Alaska's Resurrection Bay to see the drone in action*.

* vehicle　測定媒体
* test　検査する
* at a time　一度に
* was deployed
　配置された
* the Gulf of Alaska
　アラスカ湾
* The Associated
　Press
　AP通信（アメリカ
　の通信社）
* in action　作業中の

STEP 1　内容理解前に、文字を追いながらモデル音声をまねてシャドーイングしましょう。

Main Topics　1〜3の主旨について下記の空欄を埋めましょう。

1. A drone was used for the first time to measure (　　　　　　　　) in the ocean.
2. The drone can operate at 1,000 meters underwater (　　　　　　　　) at a time.
3. This research was done to investigate (　　　　　) climate change affects the ocean's chemistry.

内容を理解したら、次の各 STEP に注意しながらシャドーイングしましょう。

STEP 2 🄢 Shadowing Tips 【句強勢】

意味的・文法的なまとまりとなっている句は一気に発音します。**句の中には強勢が置かれて強く長く発音される部分**と、弱く短く発音される部分が出てきます。

Ex. 1 l. 2-3. It is believed / to be the first time / such a vehicle / has been used ....

（スラッシュは句のまとまり、●は強勢のあるところ）

STEP 3　意味を考えながらシャドーイングしましょう。

STEP 4　文法や語彙にも注意しながらシャドーイングしましょう。

> STEP 3, 4 では
> できるだけ
> 文字を見ないで！

☑ Self-Check　How was your shadowing?

😄 Great!	🙂 Good!	😐 Not too bad!	😰 Tough!

4 The team says the project could be a major (¹   ) (²   ) in measuring the environmental health of oceans. The scientists are most (³   ) in levels of ocean acidification. This happens when CO_2 emissions in the atmosphere (⁴   ) their (⁵   ) into the ocean. Ocean acidification can harm or kill some kinds of (⁶   ) (⁷   ).

5 Scientists have linked CO_2 emissions to* global warming (⁸   ) by human activities.

6 In a way*, oceans have done humans a big favor* by (⁹   ) (¹⁰   ) some of the CO_2. If this were (¹¹   ) (¹²   ) (¹³   ), there would be much more CO_2 in the atmosphere. This would trap* more of the (¹⁴   ) (¹⁵   ) and further warm the Earth.

7 "But the problem is now that the ocean is (¹⁶   ) its chemistry because of this uptake," said team member Claudine Hauri. She is an oceanographer* with the International Arctic Research Center* at the University of Alaska Fairbanks*.

* linked ～ to ...
～を…と関連させる
* in a way
ある意味では
* have done humans
a big favor
人類のために非常に役立ってきた
* trap　取り込む
* oceanographer
海洋学者
* the International
Arctic Research
Center　国際北極圏研究センター
* the University of
Alaska Fairbanks
アラスカ大学フェアバンクス

Main Topics　④ ～ ⑦ の主旨について下記の空欄を埋めましょう。

4 Scientists are concerned about levels of (   ). As oceans absorb CO_2, the acidification (   ) and might cause damage or (   ) the life of the ocean.

5 CO_2 emissions are related to (   ).

6 (   ) is reduced because it is absorbed by the oceans. Otherwise, global warming would speed up.

7 This uptake causes the problem of the changing (   ).

\\ Let's Try Shadowing Again! //

News 全体または一部のシャドーイングを行いましょう。

➡️ Comprehension

A Answer the questions.

	Climate Change
In the air	1. What is one of the causes of climate change? ( ) 2. Why are levels of CO_2 in the air reduced? ( )
In the ocean	3. How do CO_2 emissions affect oceans? ( ) 4. How does ocean acidification affect oceans? ( )

B Vocabulary: Choose the appropriate word. Change the form if necessary.

1. Too much drinking can severely (   ) your health.
2. The company will open a new showroom for their motor (   ).
3. Read the instructions on how to (   ) the machine before using it.
4. The snowstorm last month (   ) severe damage to this region's infrastructure.
5. Would you (   ) me for a new suit?

> cause / vehicles / measure / affect / operate

Summary of the News   Choose the appropriate word.

Drones can (1.   ) down to 1,000 meters (2.   ) and are used to examine the levels of ocean acidification. Some of the CO_2 is (3.   ) in the ocean, and this (4.   ) to the control of climate change. However, the problem is that this (5.   ) is changing the (6.   ) of the ocean.

> uptake / dive / chemistry / absorbed / underwater / contributes

Let's Talk — Talk about why it is important to monitor CO_2 levels in the ocean.

Underwater Drone Measures Ocean Carbon Levels

Chapter 2

Warm-up

1. If you had a drone, what would you do with it?

2. How do you think a drone examines CO_2 levels in the ocean?

3. How do you think CO_2 emissions affect the ocean's ecosystem?

4. How do rising sea water temperatures affect the ocean?

🔑 Key Words and Phrases   Choose the proper meaning.

- ( ) CO_2 measurements
- ( ) drone's sensor
- ( ) a temperature-controlled system
- ( ) accurate
- ( ) similar robotic gliders

① 正確な
② ドローンのセンサー
③ CO_2 測定値
④ 同じようなロボットのグライダー
⑤ 温度管理されたシステム

\\ First Listening // 🎧 13 Slow 🎧 14 Natural

まず何も見ないで News の始まり部分を聞きましょう。どれくらい理解できましたか。

About 　　　 %

それでは次のページで文字を見ながらもう一度聞きましょう。

\\ **Let's Try Shadowing!** // 🎧13 Slow 🎧14 Natural

1. One of the best ways to measure ocean acidification is to collect CO_2 measurements. Until now, these collections were mostly done from ships or with floating devices at the ocean surface or equipment on the ocean floor.

2. Hauri is working with another researcher, Andrew McDonnell, on the project. He is an oceanographer with the College of Fisheries and Ocean Sciences* at the university.

3. The two – who are married – teamed up in recent months with engineers from Cyprus Subsea Consulting and Services*, which provided the drone. A German company, 4H-Jena, supplied the CO_2 sensor. The team repeatedly took the drone farther and farther* into Resurrection Bay from the coastal community of Seward to carry out the tests.

* the College of Fisheries and Ocean Sciences
水産海洋学部

* Cyprus Subsea Consulting and Services
キプロスの環境コンサルタント

* farther and farther
どんどん離れたところへ

STEP 1 内容理解前に、文字を追いながらモデル音声をまねてシャドーイングしましょう。

Main Topics   1 〜 3 の主旨について下記の空欄を埋めましょう。

1. Levels of ocean acidification are examined by (
). This was done from ships or equipment on the bottom of the ocean.
2. The researchers on the project are (   ).
3. The research team took the drone far off (   ) to do (   ).

内容を理解したら、次の各 STEP に注意しながらシャドーイングしましょう。

STEP 2 **Shadowing Tips**【文強勢（リズム）】

▶ 英語と日本語はリズムに違いがあります。英語では、1文の中に強勢を受ける語と受けない語があり、**強勢を受ける音節が時間的に等間隔に現れます。**

Ex. 1 ll. 2-4. these collections were mostly dóne from shíps or with flóating

devices at the ocean súrface... (●は強勢を受けるところ)

▶ collections から done、done から ships、ships から floating、floating から surface はほぼ同じ時間をかけて発話します。

STEP 3 意味を考えながらシャドーイングしましょう。

STEP 4 文法や語彙にも注意しながらシャドーイングしましょう。

> STEP 3, 4 では
> できるだけ
> 文字を見ないで！

☑ **Self-Check** How was your shadowing?

😄 Great!	🙂 Good!	😐 Not too bad!	😞 Tough!

④ Researchers said the drone's sensor is like a very small laboratory. It examines CO_2 data and (¹   ) it inside a temperature-controlled system.

⑤ Richard Feely is a scientist with the U.S. National Oceanic and Atmospheric Administration (NOAA)*. He is stationed at the agency's Pacific Marine Environmental Laboratory* in Seattle, Washington.

⑥ Feely said the goal of the project is (²   ) (³   ) the measurements collected by the glider just (⁴   ) (⁵   ) (⁶   ) those carried out on ships.

⑦ Researchers in Canada have also tested a (⁷   ) CO_2 measuring (⁸   ) attached to a drone. But that sensor (⁹   ) (¹⁰   ) (¹¹   ) (¹²   ) effective targets for ocean acidification observations*.

⑧ McDonnell said his goal is to one day have a large number of similar robotic gliders (¹³   ) in oceans across the world. Such efforts will be important in helping scientists "understand much more about (¹⁴   ) (¹⁵   ) (¹⁶   ) in the ocean than we have before," he said.

* the U.S. National Oceanic and Atmospheric Administration (NOAA)
アメリカ海洋大気庁

* Pacific Marine Environmental Laboratory
太平洋海洋環境研究所

* effective targets for ocean acidification observations
海洋酸性化レベルの観測に有効な測定基準

Main Topics ④ 〜 ⑧ の主旨について下記の空欄を埋めましょう。

④ (   ) examines CO_2 data and saves it in a temperature-controlled system.

⑤ One of the researchers is working at the agency's (   ).

⑥ The project aims to improve the glider's (   ) to match the accuracy of (   ) measurements.

⑦ Another test was carried out with a smaller (   ) attached to a drone, but it has failed to meet the required standards.

⑧ In the future, if lots of similar drones work underwater around the world, scientists can (   ) what is happening in the ocean.

＼＼ **Let's Try Shadowing Again!** ／／
News 全体または一部のシャドーイングを行いましょう。

➤ Comprehension

A Answer the questions.

The Project	
Method	1. How do researchers measure ocean acidification? ( ) 2. Where are the tests repeatedly done? ( ) 3. What does the drone's sensor do? ( )
Purpose	4. What is the purpose of the project? ( )
Expectation	5. Why is it good to use lots of similar drones in all the oceans? ( )

B Vocabulary: Choose the appropriate word(s). Change the form if necessary.

1. You should (   ) the details before signing the contract.
2. Applicants should make sure a photo is (   ) to their resume.
3. Dairy products must be (   ) at a low temperature.
4. The consultant (   ) our company with financial advice yesterday.
5. We will (   ) a survey on consumer preference for our new beverage.

provide / attach / examine / carry out / store

Summary of the News   Choose the appropriate word.

Ocean (1.   ) is measured by (2.   ) CO_2 measurements. The goal of this project using the drone is to collect CO_2 measurements as (3.   ) as it is done on ships. If similar types of drones work (4.   ) around the world, researchers understand (5.   ) of what is (6.   ) in the ocean.

happening / acidification / more / accurately / underwater / collecting

Let's Talk ← Talk about the attempts of scientists to measure CO_2 levels in the ocean using various methods.

Study: Climate Change Likely to Increase Virus Spread in Animals

Chapter 1

Warm-up

1. What do you think about the relation between viruses and temperature?

2. Did you know that climate change might accelerate the pace of virus growth?

3. How many mammals do you know?

Key Words and Phrases   Choose the proper meaning.

- (　) climate change
- (　) new viruses to spread
- (　) the risk of new disease
- (　) pass from animals to humans
- (　) a temperature rise
- (　) cross-species virus
- (　) infectious disease

① 動物から人へ感染する
② 異種間で感染するウイルス
③ 新しいウイルスの拡散
④ 新しい病気が起こるリスク
⑤ 気温上昇
⑥ 感染症
⑦ 気候変動

\\ First Listening // 🎧17 Slow 🎧18 Natural

まず何も見ないで News の始まり部分を聞きましょう。どれくらい理解できましたか。

About ☐ %

それでは次のページで文字を見ながらもう一度聞きましょう。

\\ Let's Try Shadowing! // 🎧17 Slow 🎧18 Natural

1. A new study predicts that climate change will cause thousands of new viruses* to spread among many kinds of animals by 2070. The researchers say such spread will likely increase the risk of new diseases that pass from animals to humans.

2. The research covered about 3,000 kinds of mammals, animals including cats, bats, whales, and humans, to name a few*. The scientists created a model to see how these species might migrate* and share viruses in the next 50 years if the world warms by 2 degrees Celsius*. Recent research has suggested that such a temperature rise is possible.

* viruses
  ウイルス virus の複数形

* to name a few
  一部の例を挙げると

* migrate　移動する
* Celsius　摂氏

STEP 1 内容理解前に、文字を追いながらモデル音声をまねてシャドーイングしましょう。

Main Topics　1 ～ 2 の主旨について下記の空欄を埋めましょう。

1. A new study shows the (　　　　　　　　　　) risk of new diseases to be transmitted to humans through animals due to (　　　　　　　　　　).

2. Recent research made a model that showed how a temperature (　　　　) of 2 degrees Celsius would influence sharing (　　　　　　) among different (　　　　　　) in next 50 years.

内容を理解したら、次の各 **STEP** に注意しながらシャドーイングしましょう。

STEP 2 **Shadowing Tips** 【文強勢（重要な部分を強調）】

▶ 文の中で強勢を受ける語は、伝えたい重要な部分です。日本語を第1言語とする人の英語の発音は平板になりがちですが、**伝えたい部分を強調して発音**すれば、メリハリのきいたリズミカルな発音になります。強調されやすいのは、動詞、名詞、形容詞、副詞、疑問詞、数詞などの内容語です。

Ex. 1 ll. 1-3.　climate change will cause thousands of new viruses to spread among many kinds of animals by 2070.

STEP 3 意味を考えながらシャドーイングしましょう。

STEP 4 文法や語彙にも注意しながらシャドーイングしましょう。

> STEP 3, 4 では
> できるだけ
> 文字を見ないで！

☑ Self-Check　How was your shadowing?

😄 Great!	🙂 Good!	😐 Not too bad!	😣 Tough!

≡⟶ Fill in the Blanks 🎧 19 Slow 🎧 20 Natural

③ The team said the model predicted that cross-species virus spread will happen (¹   ) (²   ) 4,000 times among mammals.

④ The researchers said (³   ) (⁴   ) viruses will spread to humans or lead to widespread pandemics* like COVID-19*. However, the study suggests that the high number of cross-species viruses will increase the risk (⁵   ) (⁶   ) to humans.

⑤ The findings recently appeared in the publication *Nature*.

⑥ The study points to two major worldwide crises* that could cause diseases to (⁷   ) (⁸   ) from animals to humans – climate change and infectious disease spread.

⑦ Past research has looked at how deforestation*, the disappearance of species and the wildlife trade (⁹   ) (¹⁰   ) (¹¹   ) animal-human disease spread. But there has been (¹²   ) (¹³   ) (¹⁴   ) how climate change could influence this kind of disease spread, the researchers said.

⑧ "We don't talk about climate a lot in the context of* zoonoses*," said study co-writer* Colin Carlson, a professor of biology at Georgetown University* in Washington D.C. Zoonoses is a term for diseases (¹⁵   ) (¹⁶   ) spread from animals to people. "Our study ... brings together the two most pressing* global crises we have," Carlson added.

* pandemics　深刻な感染の世界的大流行
* COVID-19　コロナウイルス感染症

* *Nature*　科学技術を中心とする国際的な学術誌
* crises　危機 crisis の複数形
* deforestation　森林破壊

* in the context of　〜という観点から
* zoonoses は複数形　単数形は zoonosis
* study co-writer　共同研究者
* Georgetown University　ジョージタウン大学
* pressing　差し迫った

Main Topics　③〜⑧ の主旨について下記の空欄を埋めましょう。

③ The research (   ) predicted that cross-species virus spread might occur over 4000 times.

④ As happened with (   ), cross-species viruses could spread to (   ).

⑤ The (   ) appeared in *Nature*.

⑥ Two major (   ) are: climate change and infectious disease spread.

⑦ Little research has been done on the (   ) between (   ) and cross-species virus (   ).

⑧ Carlson says their study focuses on how (   ) could influence zoonoses.

＼＼ Let's Try Shadowing Again! ／／　News 全体または一部のシャドーイングを行いましょう。

⟹ Comprehension

A Fill in the blanks.

Event / Person	Occurrence Regarding Climate Change	Condition
A new Study	forecast that climate change will cause a large number of (1.) to (2.) among various kinds of animals	by (3.).
The team of scientists	made a model to see how approximately 3,000 kinds of mammals might (4.) viruses in (5.) years	if the world warms (6.) Celsius.
The model	predicted (7.) would happen more than 4,000 times among mammals.	
Less research	has been done on (8.) climate change could (9.) this kind of disease spread.	
Colin Carlson	said the team investigates the relation of the two most pressing global crises: (10.) and (11.).	

B Vocabulary: Choose the appropriate word. Change the form if necessary.
1. Sometimes a black cat (   ) in a mystery story.
2. My teacher (   ) I study abroad last year.
3. AI experts have been (   ) computer viruses for years.
4. We must not (   ) any conflict with other countries.
5. Mr. Black is so stubborn that he has never (   ) his opinion.

risk / appear / change / research / suggest

Summary of the News Choose the appropriate word.

A new study (1.   ) in *Nature* showed the possibility of the (2.   ) risk of new disease (3.   ) from animals to humans due to climate change. Especially, cross-species viruses will make spread to humans more (4.   ). The team will (5.   ) research on the association between climate change and (6.   ) disease spread.

infectious / passing / published / frequent / further / increased

👄 **Let's Talk** — Talk about the future possible pandemics due to the increased risk of cross-species virus transmission.

Study: Climate Change Likely to Increase Virus Spread in Animals

Chapter 2

Warm-up

1. Had you ever worried about the influence of viruses before the pandemic COVID-19 began?

2. What do you do to protect yourself from being infected?

3. What do you think is the world's most dangerous animal that can cause death to humans?

🔑 Key Words and Phrases   Choose the proper meaning.

- (　) a warming planet
- (　) this particular contribution
- (　) conservative estimate
- (　) suspicions
- (　) greater frequency
- (　) climate-driven
- (　) not preventable

① 控えめな予測
② 疑念（うすうす気づいていること）
③ 温暖化する地球
④ かなり高い頻度
⑤ 気候変動に起因する
⑥ この研究の出版本（投稿）
⑦ 避けられない

\\ First Listening // 🎧21 Slow 🎧22 Natural

まず何も見ないで News の始まり部分を聞きましょう。
どれくらい理解できましたか。

About ☐ %

それでは次のページで文字を見ながらもう一度聞きましょう。 ➡

\\ Let's Try Shadowing! // 🎧21 Slow 🎧22 Natural

1. Many experts on climate change and infectious disease agree that a warming planet will likely lead to increased risk that new viruses will be created.

2. Daniel R. Brooks is a biologist at the University of Nebraska State Museum* and co-author of the book *The Stockholm Paradigm: Climate Change and Emerging Disease*. He told The Associated Press that the latest study supports the idea that new disease threats can be linked to climate change.

3. "This particular contribution is an extremely conservative estimate" for possible new infectious disease spread caused by climate change, Brooks said.

* the University of Nebraska State Museum
ネブラスカ州立大学自然史博物館

* *The Stockholm Paradigm: Climate Change and Emerging Disease*
2019年出版された書籍名

STEP 1　内容理解前に、文字を追いながらモデル音声をまねてシャドーイングしましょう。

Main Topics　1〜3の主旨について下記の空欄を埋めましょう。

1. It is a common understanding among (　　　　　　　) on climate change and infectious disease that global (　　　　　　　) could be the cause of the rise of (　　　　　　　).

2. According to Brooks, the latest (　　　　　　) admits that the risk of new disease can be associated with (　　　　　　　).

3. Brooks also said the idea supported by the latest study is a low (　　　　　　).

内容を理解したら、次の各 **STEP** に注意しながらシャドーイングしましょう。

STEP 2 **Shadowing Tips** 【リズム】

文の強調したい語を発音するときは、メリハリをつけて、**強調したい語はゆっくり言い**、それ以外の語は速く言うようにしましょう。

Ex. 1 l. 2-3.　a warming planet will likely lead to increased risk that new viruses will be created

STEP 3　意味を考えながらシャドーイングしましょう。

STEP 4　文法や語彙にも注意しながらシャドーイングしましょう。

> STEP 3, 4 ではできるだけ文字を見ないで！

☑ Self-Check　How was your shadowing?

😄 Great!	🙂 Good!	😐 Not too bad!	😟 Tough!

⇒ Fill in the Blanks 🎧 23 Slow 🎧 24 Natural

4 Aaron Bernstein is a medical doctor and (^{1})
(^{2}) of the Center for Climate, Health, and the Global
Environment* at Harvard University's T.H. Chan School of
Public Health*. He said the study (^{3}) (^{4})
suspicions about the effects planet warming can have
(^{5}) (^{6}) creation of new infectious diseases.

5 He noted that the study suggests such cases "may already
(^{7}) (^{8}) with greater frequency and in
places (^{9}) (^{10}) many people live."

6 Study co-writer Gregory Albery is a disease expert at
Georgetown University. He told the AP that because climate-
driven infectious diseases are likely already (^{11})
(^{12}), the world should be doing more to (^{13})
(^{14}) and prepare (^{15}) (^{16}).

7 "It's not preventable, even in the best case climate change
scenarios," Albery said.

* the Center for Climate, Health, and the Global Environment (C-CHANGE) 気候・健康・地球環境研究センター

* Harvard University's T.H. Chan School of Public Health ハーバード大学 T.H.Chan 公衆衛生大学院

Main Topics   4 〜 7 の主旨について下記の空欄を埋めましょう。

4 Bernstein said the study clarified (
) on the creation of new infectious diseases.

5 Bernstein also said that the creation of new diseases may already be happening in
areas (   ).

6 Albery, the study co-writer, warned that all of us should prepare for the situation
where (   )
have already been created.

7 Albery said the impact of climate change is not (   ).

＼＼ Let's Try Shadowing Again! ／／

News 全体または一部のシャドーイングを行いましょう。

⇒ Comprehension

A Fill in the blanks (1, 2) and choose the proper answer (3, 4, and 5).

Name	Profession	Statement	Option
(1.)	biologist	He said their latest study modestly points out the impact of climate change on (3.).	a. the effects planet warming can have on the creation of new infectious diseases
Aaron Bernstein	(2.)	The phrase "such cases" in Bernstein's suggestion refers to (4.).	b. climate change that is happening slower than expected
Aaron Bernstein	disease expert	Albery's words "the best case climate change scenarios" mean (5.).	c. possible new infectious diseases spread

B Vocabulary: Choose the appropriate word. Change the form if necessary.

1. Let's all work together, whether (   ) or liberal.
2. Clicking on a (   ) sent to you by someone you don't know is dangerous.
3. It is difficut to predict the (   ) of earthquakes in specified areas.
4. We would like to (   ) that your shipment has arrived safely.
5. It is essential for businesses to (   ) a good working environment for their employees.

> confirm / conservative / link / create / frequency

Summary of the News   Choose the appropriate word.

The new study (1.   ) many experts (2.   ) the fact that global warming will lead to (3.   ) risk of creation of new viruses. Bernstein, director of C-CHANGE, said the (4.   ) of the new study is (5.   ). Study co-writer Gregory Albery admits that climate-driven infectious diseases have already (6.   ).

> increased / acknowledge / makes / argument / valid / appeared

 **Let's Talk** — Talk about the experts' comments on how climate change can increase the risk of creating new viruses.

Scientists Discover Compound in Corals Shown to Fight Cancer

Chapter 1

Warm-up

1. Have you ever seen this thing shown in the picture above? What is it?

2. Have you ever heard about medical uses of sea creatures?

3. Can you guess what elements of this sea creature are used to treat cancer?

🔑 Key Words and Phrases   Choose the proper meaning.

- (　) compound
- (　) a chemical
- (　) sea corals
- (　) cancer
- (　) substance
- (　) treatments
- (　) medical uses
- (　) cancer-fighting properties

① 医療用途
② 癌と闘う特性
③ 海珊瑚
④ 治療
⑤ 癌
⑥ 化学物質
⑦ 物質
⑧ 化合物

\\\\ First Listening //   🎧 25 Slow   🎧 26 Natural

まず何も見ないで News の始まり部分を聞きましょう。どれくらい理解できましたか。

About [　　] %

それでは次のページで文字を見ながらもう一度聞きましょう。

\\ Let's Try Shadowing! // 🎧 **25** Slow 🎧 **26** Natural

1. Researchers say they have discovered a chemical found in sea corals that could be effective in treating cancer.
2. Scientists had been searching for the compound for more than 25 years after early studies in the 1990s suggested it could slow cancer cell growth. A researcher finally discovered the substance in a common kind of soft coral* off the coast of* the American state of Florida.
3. A research team from the University of Utah* has confirmed the discovery. The team said their results could lead to widespread production of the substance for use in cancer drugs.
4. The use of natural substances to treat disease is not new, NOAA* reports. Compounds from all kinds of organisms have long been studied and tested as possible treatments for many health conditions.

* soft coral
  軟質サンゴ（骨格は
  あるが細かい骨片の
  サンゴ）
* off the coast of
  ～の沖で
* the University of
  Utah
  ユタ大学（アメリカ
  合衆国ユタ州）
* NOAA: the U.S.
  National Oceanic
  and Atmospheric
  Administration

STEP 1 　内容理解前に、文字を追いながらモデル音声をまねてシャドーイングしましょう。

Main Topics 　1〜4の主旨について下記の空欄を埋めましょう。

1. Researchers found (　　　　　　　　　　) which is effective in treating cancer.
2. About 25 years ago, it was suggested that the chemical (
   　　　　　) of cancer cells.
3. Researchers certified the possibility of use of the (　　　　　　　) in cancer drugs.
4. (　　　　　　　　　　　) from various (　　　　　　　　) have
   been used as potential (　　　　　　　) for health conditions.

　　　　　内容を理解したら、次の各 **STEP** に注意しながらシャドーイングしましょう。

STEP 2 **Shadowing Tips** 【イントネーション】

▶ 日本語を第1言語とする人の英語発音の特徴として、単語やフレーズごとに音を下げる傾向があります。しかし英語のイントネーション（音の高低）では、**フレーズの終わりでも同じ高さを保ったまま、あるいは少し上昇して次のフレーズに続く**ことがよくあります。

　Ex. 1 l.1-2. they have discovered→ a chemical→ found in sea corals↗ that could be
　　　　　effective in treating↗ cancer.

▶ ここでは sea corals の後ろでは音が少し上昇して、次の that ... に続いています。

STEP 3 　意味を考えながらシャドーイングしましょう。

STEP 4 　文法や語彙にも注意しながらシャドーイングしましょう。

（吹き出し）STEP 3, 4 では
できるだけ
文字を見ないで！

☑ Self-Check 　How was your shadowing?

😆 Great!	🙂 Good!	😐 Not too bad!	😵 Tough!

⇒ Fill in the Blanks 🎧 27 Slow 🎧 28 Natural

5 Since many corals stay in one place, they have developed chemical defenses* to protect against other (¹   ) (²   ) sea life that could threaten them, NOAA reports. Scientists study such chemicals in (³   ) (⁴   ) to find effective medical uses.

6 But a major barrier to those efforts has been the difficulty of gathering (⁵   ) (⁶   ) these compounds to carry out effective research.

7 The chemical (⁷   ) (⁸   ) the latest study is called eleutherobin*. It was discovered in soft corals near Australia. Scientists reported in the 1990s that the chemical had cancer-fighting properties.

8 Researchers involved in the study said the chemical can play (⁹   ) (¹⁰   ) in breaking down important cell structures*. It is used by soft corals (¹¹   ) (¹²   ) defense against predators*. But scientific studies have suggested the compound also shows promise* in reducing cancer cell growth.

9 The studies led scientists to keep searching for large (¹³   ) (¹⁴   ) the chemical that would be necessary to (¹⁵   ) (¹⁶   ) additional testing and possibly develop new cancer drugs. But those efforts were unsuccessful for many years.

---

* chemical defenses
細菌の細胞壁を壊す
酵素による自己防御

* eleutherobin
サンゴから分離した
天然物質（エリュテ
ロビン）

* cell structures
細胞構造

* predators
捕食動物

* show promise
有望である

Main Topics   5 ～ 9 の主旨について下記の空欄を埋めましょう。

5 Scientists study (   ) from (   ) as potential medical treatments.

6 The main (   ) is the challenge of obtaining sufficient (   ).

7 The chemical eleutherobin, found in (   ) near Australia, has anticancer (   ).

8 The studies suggest the (   ) has the potential to (   ) cancer cell growth.

9 Scientists' efforts to find (   ) quantities of the chemical have not been (   ) for a long time.

\\\ Let's Try Shadowing Again! //

News 全体または一部のシャドーイングを行いましょう。

34

➡️ Comprehension

A Answer the questions.

The Project		
In the 1990s	1. What did the study in the 1990s show? (	)
For over 25 years	2. What have researchers done to develop cancer medicines? (	)
	3. What has been a challenge for them? (	)
News release	4. Where was the coral with the special compound found? (	)
In the future	5. How will the substance discovered by the research team be used? (	)

B Vocabulary: Choose the appropriate word. Change the form if necessary.

1. The nurse (   ) the patient's chills with a warm blanket yesterday.
2. I need to (   ) for my keys before leaving the house.
3. With sufficient water and sunlight, the plant's (   ) was impressive.
4. You can (   ) your head during bike rides by wearing a helmet.
5. Bears in the forest may occasionally (   ) human safety.

> growth / protect / search / threaten / treat

Summary of the News Choose the appropriate word.

Studies from the 1990s showed that the (1.   ) found in corals may (2.   ) the growth of cancer cells. Scientists have been (3.   ) for it, hoping to use it to study cancer (4.   ) and (5.   ) drugs. The compound was recently found in a common soft coral (6.   ) the coast of Florida.

> treatments / slow / searching / produce / off / chemical

Let's Talk — Talk about the discovery of the chemical found in sea corals that could be effective in treating cancer.

Scientists Discover Compound in Corals Shown to Fight Cancer

Chapter 2

Warm-up

1. What does DNA stand for?

2. Did you know that the number of marine creatures is rapidly decreasing?

3. Can you think of other natural substances which are good for our health?

🔑 Key Words and Phrases   Choose the proper meaning.

- (　) organisms
- (　) theory
- (　) genetic code
- (　) DNA
- (　) instructions
- (　) bacteria
- (　) laboratory
- (　) manufacture

① 理論・見解
② 指示・命令
③ 製造する
④ 実験室
⑤ 細菌
⑥ 有機体・生物
⑦ 遺伝情報
⑧ デオキシリボ核酸（遺伝子を持つ物質）

\\\\ First Listening //   🎧 **29** Slow   🎧 **30** Natural

まず何も見ないで News の始まり部分を聞きましょう。どれくらい理解できましたか。

About 　　　 %

それでは次のページで文字を見ながらもう一度聞きましょう。 ➤

\\ **Let's Try Shadowing!** // 🎧 **29** Slow 🎧 **30** Natural

1. Then, a scientist working on the University of Utah team, Paul Scesa, found a soft coral in the ocean off the Florida coast that contained eleutherobin.

2. The team sought to* find out whether the corals made the chemical themselves or whether it was produced by symbiotic* organisms living inside the corals. Scesa said in a statement it did not "make sense*" to him that the compound would only be produced by other organisms.

3. His team knew, for example, that some soft corals do not have symbiotic organisms and yet their bodies contain the same collection of chemicals.

* sought to
　～しようと努めた

* symbiotic　共生の

* make sense
　筋が通っている

STEP 1 ▶ 　内容理解前に、文字を追いながらモデル音声をまねてシャドーイングしましょう。

Main Topics 　1 ～ 3 の主旨について下記の空欄を埋めましょう。

1. The coral found off the (　　　　　　) coast (　　　　　　) a chemical, eleutherobin.

2. The team investigated the origin of the (　　　　　　) eleutherobin found in soft coral, questioning if it was produced by the (　　　　　) or (　　　　　　　) living inside the corals.

3. Even though some soft corals don't have (　　　　　　　　　), they still have the same special (　　　　　) in their bodies.

内容を理解したら、次の各 **STEP** に注意しながらシャドーイングしましょう。

STEP 2 ▶ Shadowing Tips 【音声変化（消える音 [t] [t]）】

英語では、音は多様な変化をします。その1つに単語の一部がほとんど聞こえない場合があります。2 l.1 sought to の sought の語末の [t] と to の語頭の [t] のように、**同じ発音の子音が続くときは前の単語の子音が聞こえない**ことがよくあります。「ソート・トゥ」ではなく「ソー・トゥ」のように聞こえます。

STEP 3 ▶ 　意味を考えながらシャドーイングしましょう。

STEP 4 ▶ 　文法や語彙にも注意しながらシャドーイングしましょう。

> STEP 3, 4 では
> できるだけ
> 文字を見ないで！

☑ Self-Check 　How was your shadowing?

😄 Great!	🙂 Good!	😐 Not too bad!	😫 Tough!

≡▷ Fill in the Blanks 🎧 31 Slow 🎧 32 Natural

4 To test their theory, the researchers attempted to* (^{1}) (^{2}) how the corals were producing the compound. To do this, they needed to study the corals' genetic code to learn (^{3}) (^{4}) included instructions on how to produce the chemical.

5 This process is possible through modern (^{5}) (^{6}) studying the DNA* of organisms.

6 The next step was difficult because the scientists did not know what the instructions for making the chemical (^{7}) (^{8}) like.

7 But they reported they were able to identify (^{9}) (^{10}) DNA in the coral that were very close* to genetic instructions* for similar compounds (^{11}) (^{12}) species. They were then able to provide those instructions to bacteria grown (^{13}) (^{14}) laboratory. The team reported that the bacterial microorganisms* were able to copy the first steps of making eleutherobin.

8 The researchers say their experiments demonstrated that it should be possible to manufacture the chemical in the laboratory. This could (^{15}) (^{16}) possible widespread production of new anti-cancer drugs.

---

* attempted to
　～しようと試みた

* DNA
　Deoxyribonucleic
　Acid

* close　そっくりな
* genetic instructions
　親と同じものを作る
　遺伝情報を指令する
　遺伝的命令

* microorganisms
　微生物

Main Topics　4 ～ 8 の主旨について下記の空欄を埋めましょう。

4 Scientist studied corals' (   ) to find their instructions on how to produce the chemical.

5 Scientists used advanced (   ) to study the corals' DNA.

6 The next step, to discover (   ) instructions, was difficult.

7 Scientists found parts of (   ) corresponding to instructions for making similar (   ), and grew lab-grown (   ), which started making eleutherobin.

8 Researchers' (   ) showed that it's possible to make the chemical in a lab, which leads to the potential for wide-scale (   ) of new anti-cancer medications.

＼＼ Let's Try Shadowing Again! ／／

News 全体または一部のシャドーイングを行いましょう。

➤ Comprehension

A Choose the proper answer.

Process	What Happened?
Discovery	A scientist found (1.)
Inquiry	The research team tried to clarify (2.)
	The research team knew that (3.)
	Scientists examined (4.)
Identification	Scientists found (5.)
Replication	Scientists used (6.)

a. some corals without symbiotic organisms had similar chemicals.
b. whether the coral or symbiotic organisms produced the chemical.
c. genetic instructions for making the chemical in the coral's DNA.
d. a chemical called eleutherobin in a soft coral off the Florida coast.
e. bacteria to copy the instructions and make the chemical.
f. the coral's DNA to find out how it produced the chemical.

B Vocabulary: Choose the appropriate word. Change the form if necessary.

1. The (   ) is full of colorful fish and friendly sea turtles.
2. A complex mechanism (   ) the machine demands careful maintenance.
3. His (   ) shocked everyone.
4. The advanced technology in our (   ) world offers us great convenience.
5. You can (   ) the bird by its different feather colors.

> identify / inside / modern / ocean / statement

Summary of the News   Choose the appropriate word(s).

The research team at the University of Utah investigated how eleutherobin in a coral (1.   ) using DNA analysis. They (2.   ) parts of DNA that were similar to (3.   ) in other species. They successfully (4.   ) eleutherobin in the laboratory, which may lead to the (5.   ) of new (6.   ) drugs.

> anti-cancer / replicated / genetic instructions / identified / production / grows

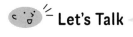 **Let's Talk** — Talk about how researchers found the way to produce an effective chemical to fight cancer.

Unit 9

Music Groups Try Making Performances Better for the Environment

Chapter 1

Warm-up

1. Who do you think the people in the photo are?

2. What are they doing? For what?

3. Re-read the title of this unit. What are music groups trying to do? Why, and how?

🔑 **Key Words and Phrases**   Choose the proper meaning.

- ( ) power
- ( ) sustainable
- ( ) energy-storing
- ( ) produce electricity
- ( ) competitions
- ( ) business model
- ( ) reduce the effects of

① 電気を作り出す
② 電力
③ 競争
④ …の影響を減らす
⑤ 環境を壊さず利用可能な
⑥ 企業の戦略
⑦ エネルギーを貯える

\\\ First Listening //   🎧 33 Slow   🎧 34 Natural

まず何も見ないで News の始まり部分を聞きましょう。どれくらい理解できましたか。

About ⬜ %

それでは次のページで文字を見ながらもう一度聞きましょう。 ➡

＼＼ Let's Try Shadowing! ／／ 🎧 33 Slow 🎧 34 Natural

① The music group Coldplay* plans to use their fans' energy to help provide power for their musical performances and to help the environment.

② The band has promised to use methods that are sustainable. This includes using energy that does not add carbon gases to the atmosphere. The band hopes to cut the amount of carbon dioxide, or CO_2, released by its business activities by 50 percent.

③ The music stars have added special dance floors and energy-storing exercise bicycles to their latest world tour. The goal is to get fans to help power the show as they dance or spin by producing electricity.

*Coldplay
イギリスの4人組
ロックバンド

STEP 1 ▶ 内容理解前に、文字を追いながらモデル音声をまねてシャドーイングしましょう。

Main Topics ①〜③ の主旨について下記の空欄を埋めましょう。

① Fans of a music group (　　　　　　　　　　) by using their energy.

② The band uses more sustainable (　　　　　　　) for their performances to reduce the emission of (　　　　).

③ Fans produce electricity by dancing or pedaling (　　　　　　　　　).

内容を理解したら、次の各 STEP▶ に注意しながらシャドーイングしましょう。

STEP 2 ▶ **Shadowing Tips** 【音声変化（消える音 [d] [t]）】

同じ発音の子音が続くときは前の単語の子音が聞こえなくなる例として、[t] が連続する場合がありました。この Unit では [d] と [t] が連続する例があります。
① l. 2 and to の [d]、③ l. 2 world tour の [d] の音はほとんど聞こえません。

STEP 3 ▶ 意味を考えながらシャドーイングしましょう。

STEP 4 ▶ 文法や語彙にも注意しながらシャドーイングしましょう。

STEP 3, 4 では
できるだけ
文字を見ないで！

☑ Self-Check How was your shadowing?

😆 Great!	🙂 Good!	😐 Not too bad!	😖 Tough!

⇒ Fill in the Blanks 🎧 35 Slow 🎧 36 Natural

4 Bassist Guy Berryman suggested music fans will be more likely (^{1} ___) (^{2} ___) changes to the concert experience if it is "a (^{3} ___) (^{4} ___) opportunity to do something fun."

5 Each special dance floor, called a kinetic dance floor*, can support many people. The floor creates electricity when people (^{5} ___) (^{6} ___) it. The band even has competitions before its performances to find out which (^{7} ___) (^{8} ___) (^{9} ___) can create the most power.

6 Each of the bikes can create (^{10} ___) (^{11} ___) (^{12} ___) 200 watts of energy, captured in batteries that run* parts of the show.

7 "Being green*... is a good business model. That's (^{13} ___) we'd like to show," said Coldplay lead singer Chris Martin. Coldplay is just one music act working to reduce the (^{14} ___) (^{15} ___) (^{16} ___) tour on the Earth's climate.

*a kinetic dance floor
再生プラスチック製の床タイルで作られたダンスフロア

*run 運営する

*green
環境問題意識の高い

Main Topics 　4 ～ 7 の主旨について下記の空欄を埋めましょう。

4 The band member believes that (___) in their shows will be accepted by their (___) as long as they are (___) things.

5 People dancing on a (___), called a kinetic dance floor, can help create (___).

6 The electricity created using bikes is stored in (___) to be used for the (___).

7 Martin is involved in a green business model to (___) the effects that musical activities have on the (___) environment.

\\ Let's Try Shadowing Again! //

News 全体または一部のシャドーイングを行いましょう。

⇒ Comprehension

A Choose the proper answer.

Who / What	What They Did	Why They Did It
Coldplay	(1.)	(2.).
Fans	(3.)	(4.).
Guy Berryman	(5.)	(6.).
Chris Martin	(7.)	(8.).

What They Did	a. believed being environmentally sustainable is a good business plan
	b. added kinetic dance floors and energy-storing exercise bikes to their tour
	c. suggested music fans will accept positive changes
	d. danced on kinetic dance floors and pedaled energy-storing exercise bikes

Why They Did It	a. to involve fans in reducing carbon emissions and to make their tour more environmentally sustainable
	b. to encourage fans to participate and enjoy the sustainable concert experience
	c. to show that being green can be a successful business and help reduce carbon emissions
	d. to produce electricity and help reduce carbon emissions during the concert

B Vocabulary: Choose the appropriate word. Change the form if necessary.

1. We can save (   ) by turning off lights when not needed.
2. Good sleep habits can improve academic (   ) for students.
3. The (   ) of homework will increase as you move up grades.
4. With a camera, you can (   ) images that become lasting memories.
5. The (   ) in this region is very hot and dry.

amount / capture / climate / energy / performance

Summary of the News   Choose the appropriate word.

Coldplay plans to make their musical performances (1.   ). During their tour, they have fans (2.   ) energy-storing bikes or dance on kinetic dance floors which create (3.   ) to power the show. The electricity created by (4.   ) helps reduce the (5.   ) of CO_2 emissions. They say being (6.   ) is a good business model.

amount / electricity / sustainable / green / pedal / fans

Let's Talk — Talk about Coldplay's plans for using fans' energy in their concerts to cut carbon emissions by 50%.

Music Groups Try Making Performances Better for the Environment

Chapter 2

Warm-up

1. Which activity would you prefer to join during a musical performance? Exercising on a bike or dancing?
2. Would you like to take part in these activities?
3. Do you know other artists who are doing environmental activities?
4. Do you have any other ideas of activities that can be done by artists?

🔑 Key Words and Phrases   Choose the proper meaning.

- (　) carbon gas emissions
- (　) a nonprofit group
- (　) plant-based
- (　) single-use
- (　) sustainable materials
- (　) recycled steel
- (　) repurposed
- (　) a sense of belonging

① 帰属意識
② 非営利団体
③ 植物由来の
④ 再利用の鋼鉄
⑤ 再利用した
⑥ 二酸化炭素の排出
⑦ 使い捨ての
⑧ 地球にやさしい素材

First Listening   🎧 37 Slow　🎧 38 Natural

まず何も見ないで News の始まり部分を聞きましょう。
どれくらい理解できましたか。

About 　　　　 %

それでは次のページで文字を見ながらもう一度聞きましょう。

\\ **Let's Try Shadowing!** // 🎧37 Slow 🎧38 Natural

1. The music artists are part of an effort by the entertainment industry — from sports teams to toy manufacturers — to reduce carbon gas emissions.

2. Adam Gardner is with Reverb*, a nonprofit group that helps bands make their concerts better for the environment. He is not involved with Coldplay's tour.

3. But Gardner said, "The relationship that musicians have with millions of their fans is unlike any other relationship of any other public figure. It can be a walking, talking* example."

4. Musicians are providing more plant-based food choices. They are not using single-use plastic containers. And they are trying to change the transportation they and their fans use.

* Reverb
音楽を通して、環境問題や社会問題に取り組む団体。環境保護運動家のLauren SullivanとミュージシャンのAdam Gardnerが2004年に設立した。

* walking, talking
気軽な

STEP 1 内容理解前に、文字を追いながらモデル音声をまねてシャドーイングしましょう。

Main Topics ①〜④の主旨について下記の空欄を埋めましょう。

1. Music artists are working with other (　　　　　　　) companies to help (　　　　　) pollution.

2. Adam Gardner works for (　　　　　　　) that supports bands in making their (　　　　　　　) more eco-friendly.

3. Gardner said that musicians have a special (　　　　　　) with their fans and they can set a good (　　　　　) of environmental activities.

4. Musicians are choosing plant-derived (　　　　) and greener (　　　　　), and not using disposable (　　　　　).

内容を理解したら、次の各 **STEP** に注意しながらシャドーイングしましょう。

STEP 2 🎵**Shadowing Tips**【音声変化（つながる音）】

自然な速度で発話される場合、意味的なつながりのある句では、**前の単語の語末の子音と次の単語の語頭の母音がひとつなぎで発音され、1つの単語のように聞こえる**ことがあります。
①l. 1 part of は「パート・オブ」というより「パートブ」、③l. 2 millions of は「ミリオンズ・オブ」というより「ミリオンゾブ」のように聞こえます。

STEP 3 意味を考えながらシャドーイングしましょう。

STEP 4 文法や語彙にも注意しながらシャドーイングしましょう。

> STEP 3, 4 では
> できるだけ
> 文字を見ないで！

☑ **Self-Check** How was your shadowing?

😄 Great!	🙂 Good!	😐 Not too bad!	😵 Tough!

5 Shawn Mendes* has promised to reduce his tour's effects on the environment and cut emissions by 50 percent for each show. He says he will use sustainable materials in tour (¹   ), stay (²   ) (³   ) that promise to cut emissions, and not use single-use plastic. He has even promised to use sustainable aircraft (⁴   ).

6 Coldplay has taken other (⁵   ) to reduce the environmental effects of its tour. The "Music of the Spheres" tour stage uses (⁶   ) steel. The band hopes to deploy the world's first tour battery system, made from 40 repurposed BMW* (⁷   ) (⁸   ) batteries. The hope is to power the entire show with batteries.

7 "We are very blessed that we have the (⁹   ) to be able to do it because it's very expensive to try these things for the first time," said Martin*.

8 Martin suggested that all of these changes are (¹⁰   ) (¹¹   ) bring a (¹²   ) (¹³   ) belonging to music fans. "Everything in our show is really designed to bring everyone into the same group. And this is just an extension of that. It makes us feel (¹⁴   ). It makes us feel (¹⁵   ) (¹⁶   ) a community," he said.

* Shawn Mendes
ショーン・メンデス
（カナダ出身のシンガーソングライター）

* BMW
ドイツの自動車メーカー

* Martin
前 Chapter で既出の Chris Martin
（Coldplay のボーカリスト）のこと

Main Topics   5 ～ 8 の主旨について下記の空欄を埋めましょう。

5 Shawn Mendes is making his tours more (   ) friendly by cutting (   ) in various ways.

6 Coldplay is using recycled (   ) for their stage and repurposed electric car batteries to minimize the (   ) impacts of their tour.

7 Chris Martin from Coldplay said that they are lucky to (   ) to make their tour eco-friendly.

8 Martin proposed that the changes are intended to create (   ) among music fans.

∖∖ Let's Try Shadowing Again! ∕∕

News 全体または一部のシャドーイングを行いましょう。

✏️ Comprehension

A Fill in the blanks.

Music Artist	Environmental Actions Taken
Coldplay	used recycled steel for the (1.), and repurposed BMW car batteries for the (2.) battery system.
Shawn Mendes	will redure emissions by 50%, will use sustainable materials for (3.), will stay at hotels with reduced emissions, and will use sustainable (4.).
Other Music Artists	provided more plant-based (5.) choices, reduced single-use (6.) containers, and changed their (7.) methods.

B Vocabulary: Choose the appropriate word. Change the form if necessary.

1. If you put in the (   ), you can achieve anything.
2. A science project can (   ) research, experimentation, and presentation of findings.
3. Bicycles are a common form of (   ) in many cities.
4. Having a balanced diet can (   ) the risk of certain diseases.
5. It took the (   ) day to fix the flat tire on his bike.

> effort / entire / involve / reduce / transportation

Summary of the News   Choose the appropriate word.

Music artists such as Martin and Mendes are working to reduce the environmental (1.   ) of their tours. They adopted (2.   ) electricity to reduce CO_2 emissions in hope of (3.   ) their fans to make more (4.   ) choices. All the (5.   ) are meant to bring a sense of (6.   ) to music fans.

> environmentally-friendly / changes / impacts / inspiring / belonging / human-powered

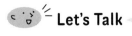 **Let's Talk** — Talk about examples of sustainable practices that musicians are adopting to reduce carbon gas emissions.

Old Clothing Gains New Popularity at Vintage Stores

Chapter 1

Warm-up

1. Have you ever bought used clothes?

2. Do you know the term "vintage store"?

3. Do you think vintage stores are popular among young people?

🔑 Key Words and Phrases   Choose the proper meaning.

- (　) gains new popularity
- (　) vintage
- (　) used clothes
- (　) sustainable
- (　) natural resources
- (　) greenhouse gas emissions
- (　) repurpose

> ① 温室効果ガスの排出
> ② 別の目的で使う
> ③ 古着
> ④ 環境を壊さず地球にやさしい
> ⑤ 天然資源
> ⑥ 古くて価値のある
> ⑦ 新たな人気を獲得する

＼＼ First Listening ／／ 🎧 41 Slow   🎧 42 Natural

まず何も見ないで News の始まり部分を聞きましょう。どれくらい理解できましたか。

About [　　　] %

それでは次のページで文字を見ながらもう一度聞きましょう。 ➡

⑉ Let's Try Shadowing! ⑉ 🎧 41 Slow 🎧 42 Natural

1 Americans in greater numbers are buying used clothing*.

2 Fans call it vintage clothing. They believe buying old, used clothes can save money. They also consider it good for the environment and stylish. Vintage stores sell clothes* from previous time periods. The stores often carry famous brands and sell them at low prices.

3 Vintage clothing has been on the rise for about 10 years. It* is driven largely by a new generation of people who are concerned about sustainable ways of living. That* means they want to waste less and use natural resources carefully.

* clothing 衣類
（集合的）不可算名詞

* clothes /klóʊ(ð)z/
（複数）衣類

* It は前出の文を指す

* That は前出の who 以
下を指す

STEP 1 ▶ 内容理解前に、文字を追いながらモデル音声をまねてシャドーイングしましょう。

Main Topics 　1 ～ 3 の主旨について下記の空欄を埋めましょう。

1 The number of Americans who buy used clothing has been (　　　　　　　　　).

2 The reasons to buy (　　　　　　　　　　) are that they are cheap, look good, and are better for the (　　　　　　　　).

3 Vintage clothing is supported by young people who care for (　　　　　　　　　　).

内容を理解したら、次の各 **STEP** に注意しながらシャドーイングしましょう。

STEP 2 🄯 Shadowing Tips 【強調】

発話は、聞き手にその話題で焦点を当てたい何かを伝えるために行います。このためすべての単語を均等に発するのではなく、**伝えたい重要な単語は長めにはっきりと発音**します。次の太字の単語は強調されています。

Ex. 1 l.1 Americans in greater numbers are buying **used** clothing.

　　 2 l.1 Fans call it **vintage** clothing. They believe buying **old**, **used** clothes can save money.

STEP 3 ▶ 意味を考えながらシャドーイングしましょう。

STEP 4 ▶ 文法や語彙にも注意しながらシャドーイングしましょう。

STEP 3, 4 では
できるだけ
文字を見ないで！

☑ Self-Check How was your shadowing?

😆 Great!	🙂 Good!	😐 Not too bad!	😣 Tough!

⟹ Fill in the Blanks 🎧 43 Slow 🎧 44 Natural

④ In (¹   ), the United Nations said that the fashion industry causes "around 10% of global greenhouse gas (²   )." The U.N.* said the industry uses more energy than the airplane and shipping industries* (³   ).

⑤ Jen Mason is the owner of Underground Vintage* in Lewes, Delaware, a town (⁴   ) the Atlantic coast*. She said that (⁵   ) in the store that do not get sold are provided (⁶   ) local people. They use the material for different purposes (⁷   ) (⁸   ) making blankets. Unsold clothes (⁹   ) go to waste*, Mason said.

⑥ "We're a coastal community. So we're always (¹⁰   ) about how to be sustainable. And we also live on a peninsula, so, you know, it (¹¹   ) a lot of resources to get stuff out and back to here*. So we're very much thinking about how to (¹²   ) something a new life."

⑦ Large fashion companies (¹³   ) beginning to join the used (¹⁴   ) movement. Levis Secondhand is a new program from Levi Strauss & Co., the blue jeans manufacturer. The program (¹⁵   ) back worn jeans* to repurpose and (¹⁶   ) them.

* The U.N.
  = the United
  Nations　国連

* shipping industries
  海運業

* Underground
  Vintage　古着店名

* the Atlantic coast
  大西洋沿岸

* go to waste
  無駄になる

* to get stuff out and
  back to here
  モノを運び出したり
  戻したりするには

* worn jeans
  はき古したジーンズ

Main Topics　④〜⑦ の主旨について下記の空欄を埋めましょう。

④ The U.N. said the volume of global greenhouse gas emissions was more from (   ) than from the airplane and shipping (   ).

⑤ Mason, the owner of a local clothing company, says they don't (   ) unsold clothes but rather (   ) for recycling purposes.

⑥ Mason said people living in a coastal community are always considering (   ).

⑦ Large fashion companies are following (   ).

＼＼ Let's Try Shadowing Again! ／／

News 全体または一部のシャドーイングを行いましょう。

➤ Comprehension

A Fill in the blanks.

Person / Group	the Trend
Many Americans	are buying (1.).
Fans of used clothing	see used clothing as (2.).
(3.) of people	want to waste (4.) and use (5.) carefully.
Vintage clothing	has been popular for about (6.).
The (7.) industry	causes around 10% of global greenhouse gas (8.).
People in a (9.) community	are thinking about how to give something (10.).
A (11.) fashion company	started a new program to buy back (12.) to (13.) and resell them.

B Vocabulary: Choose the appropriate word. Change the form if necessary.

1. We should (   ) forces and work together.
2. Many volunteers went to the disaster area to (   ) the victims.
3. It is a (   ) of money to buy a lot of unnecessary goods.
4. The bag was (   ) too expensive to sell.
5. They (   ) the company as an illegal organisation last year.

brand / price / waste / save / combine

Summary of the News   Choose the appropriate word.

Youths with high (1.   ) awareness see the (2.   ) of used clothing as (3.   ). About 10% of global greenhouse gas emissions (4.   ) from the fashion industry. (5.   ) Americans are buying used clothes. Large fashion companies are also joining the used clothing movement, which leads to a better (6.   ) of environmental conservation.

come / more / precious / reuse / sustainability / understanding

Let's Talk — Talk about some benefits of buying used clothes.

Old Clothing Gains New Popularity at Vintage Stores

Chapter 2

Warm-up

1. What are you doing to help the environment in everyday life?

2. Are you interested in vintage stores? What kind of store is favorable for you?

3. Do you like music from the 1990s and early 2000s?

🔑 Key Words and Phrases   Choose the proper meaning.

- (　) an agreement under the U.N.
- (　) looking to the past
- (　) nostalgia
- (　) different time period
- (　) physical store
- (　) some pieces that mean something

① 過去に目を向けて
② 国連での協定
③ 何かの意味があるちょっとしたもの
④ 郷愁・過去を懐かしむ心
⑤ 実店舗
⑥ 異なる時代

＼＼ First Listening ／／ 🎧 45 Slow 🎧 46 Natural

まず何も見ないで News の始まり部分を聞きましょう。どれくらい理解できましたか。

About 〔　　　〕 %

 それでは次のページで文字を見ながらもう一度聞きましょう。 ➡

Let's Try Shadowing! // 🎧 45 Slow 🎧 46 Natural

1 The Fashion Industry Charter for Climate Action* is an agreement under the U.N. to reduce greenhouse gasses. Organizations that sign the agreement promise to create fewer gasses linked to climate change. But many people buying clothing are hoping to help the environment by looking to the past.

2 A recent report in Utah's Deseret News* notes that 20th century fashion is currently the most popular in Utah's used-clothing market.

3 Delorean* 88 is a vintage store in Washington, DC. Much of the store's clothing comes from the 1990s and early 2000s. The store carries mostly t-shirts, many with band logos and sports teams. One t-shirt features* the faces of all the members of the 1996 Chicago Bulls*, including Michael Jordan and Scottie Pippen, the team's stars. Another shirt is from the rap music performer Eminem after his first album released in 1999.

* The Fashion Industry Charter for Climate Action ファッション業界気候行動憲章

* Deseret News デザレット・ニュース（アメリカ西部で最も古い出版物）

* Delorean デロリアンは1980年代の人気車の名。

* feature /fíːtʃər/ 特集する

* Chicago Bulls シカゴ・ブルズ（バスケットボールチーム）

STEP 1 内容理解前に、文字を追いながらモデル音声をまねてシャドーイングしましょう。

Main Topics 1 ～ 3 の主旨について下記の空欄を埋めましょう。

1 The fashion industry created the Fashion Industry Charter for Climate Action to
（　　　　　　　　　　　　　　　　　　　　）.

2 In Utah's used-clothing market, the recent trend in fashion is （　　　　　　　） style.

3 A vintage store named （　　　　　　　　　　　　） deals in clothing from the 1990s and early 2000s.

内容を理解したら、次の各 STEP に注意しながらシャドーイングしましょう。

STEP 2 **Shadowing Tips** 【意味グループ（発話の単位）】

長い文を発話するときは、**意味上の区切りとなるところでポーズを置きます**。次の文はスラッシュが入っているところでポーズを置きながら発話しましょう。

Ex. 1 l.1-2 The Fashion Industry Charter for Climate Action / is an agreement / under the U.N. / to reduce greenhouse gasses.

STEP 3 意味を考えながらシャドーイングしましょう。

STEP 4 文法や語彙にも注意しながらシャドーイングしましょう。

STEP 3, 4 ではできるだけ文字を見ないで！

☑ Self-Check How was your shadowing?

😄 Great!	🙂 Good!	😐 Not too bad!	😣 Tough!

⟹ Fill in the Blanks 🎧 47 Slow 🎧 48 Natural

4 Michael Diaz (¹   ) (²   ) the shop*. He said customers have (³   ) (⁴   ) and noticed shirts their parents might have had.

5 "A store like this is just — it's nostalgia for a lot of people... They'd rather have this, like a shirt⋯that has, like 10 years of history, 20 years of history — (⁵   ) (⁶   ) that over* a new shirt."

6 Mason from Underground Vintage thinks part of the popularity in vintage shopping for younger people has to do with* the time before the wide use of computers. Young people can (⁷   ) (⁸   ) the internet and visit a physical store (⁹   ) (¹⁰   ) (¹¹   ) clothes from a different time period. And the shop does not separate clothes for men and women.

7 "So that's...another way that I think that vintage shopping really (¹²   ) (¹³   ) with that generation — it's sustainable, it fits the goals of obviously having a planet (¹⁴   ) (¹⁵   ) (¹⁶   ), but also having some pieces that mean something. You know, like we say on the sign* ...wear what you like."

* the shop は前ページ
既出の Delorean 88
を指す

* over
〜より好んで

* has to do with
〜とつながりがある

* like we say on the
sign 看板に書いて
いるようにね

Main Topics   4 〜 7 の主旨について下記の空欄を埋めましょう。

4 The shop clerk Michael Diaz said customers are coming to the shop to find shirts (   ) might have worn.

5 Diaz says customers prefer (   ) items to new ones.

6 Vintage shopping is (   ) for young people because they can be away from (   ) and wear clothes from a (   ).

7 Mason says young people see (   ) as sustainable and a blessing for both the (   ) and themselves.

╲╲ Let's Try Shadowing Again! ╱╱

News 全体または一部のシャドーイングを行いましょう。

➡ Comprehension

A Complete the answers.

Group / Person	Message to deliver
Fashion organizations	What is the purpose in signing the Fashion Industry Charter for Climate Action? It is to create (1.).
Utah's Deseret News	What does its recent report announce? It notes (2.).
Michael Diaz from Delorean 88	What comments did he make? A store (3.).
Mason from Underground Vintage	What comments did he make? Vintage shopping is (4.) that mean something: (5.).

B Vocabulary: Choose the appropriate word. Change the form if necessary.

1. The eldest player put in the final (   ) in his retirement game.
2. Who is (   ) the important documents?
3. We should be especially careful about (   ) garbage.
4. He (   ) not to tell a lie, but that turned out to be a lie.
5. Don't forget to put a (   ) at the end of your sentence.

> promise / period / goal / separate / carry

Summary of the News Choose the appropriate word.

(1.   ) number of Americans, especially youths, are (2.   ) to buy used clothes. They (3.   ) it as vintage clothing. They believe that buying used ones is not (4.   ) to save money but also good for the environment. (5.   ) style fits the living pattern of people with high (6.   ) of sustainability concepts.

> a / awareness / only / regard / the / willing

Let's Talk — Talk about how vintage stores are popular among younger generations.

UN Climate Change Conference to Center on Middle East

Chapter 1

Warm-up

1. What countries are in the Middle East?

2. What do you know about the Middle East?

3. Have you ever heard of COP27?

🔑 Key Words and Phrases Choose the proper meaning.

- ( ) climate change
- ( ) COP27
- ( ) Middle East
- ( ) climate change adaptation
- ( ) clean energy production
- ( ) water scarcity

① 中東
② クリーンエネルギーの産出
③ 水不足
④ 気候変動について話し合う会議
⑤ 気候変動による影響への対処
⑥ 気候変動

＼＼ First Listening ／／ 🎧 49 Slow 🎧 50 Natural

まず何も見ないで News の始まり部分を聞きましょう。どれくらい理解できましたか。

About ☐ %

それでは次のページで文字を見ながらもう一度聞きましょう。➡

\\ **Let's Try Shadowing!** // 🎧 49 Slow 🎧 50 Natural

1. This year's United Nations climate change conference, known as COP27*, is being held in Egypt in November.
2. The conference will pay special attention to climate problems of the Middle East. The U.N. wants to talk about the damage that climate problems have already caused Middle Eastern economies.
3. Financing for climate change adaptation – the process of dealing with the effects of climate change – will be an important issue.
4. In Egypt's Nile River Delta, rising soil salt levels* are eating away* farmland. And in Afghanistan, drought has helped fuel* the movement of young people from their homes to cities in search of work.

*COP27 （2022年11月開催）COPはConference of the Partiesの頭文字、数字は第27回を表す

*soil salt levels 土壌塩分レベル
*eating away 侵食している
*fuel 活発化する

STEP 1 ▶ 内容理解前に、文字を追いながらモデル音声をまねてシャドーイングしましょう。

Main Topics 　1～4の主旨について下記の空欄を埋めましょう。

1. This year's COP27 will (　　　　　　　　) in Egypt.
2. The topic of the conference will be the damage from climate problems to (　　　　　　　　　　　).
3. Providing money to tackle the (　　　　　　　) of climate change will be (　　　　　　　　).
4. In Egypt, rising soil salt levels are reducing the amount of (　　　　　　　　), and in Afghanistan, drought has forced young people to (　　　　　) to cities searching for a job.

〜〜〜 内容を理解したら、次の各 **STEP** に注意しながらシャドーイングしましょう。 〜〜〜

STEP 2 ▶ 🄢🄗🄐🄓🄞🄦🄘🄝🄖 🅃🄘🄟🅂 【弱音（強勢を受けない音節）】

強勢を受ける部分は長く発音しますが、一方、**強勢のない部分は弱く短く発音**します。一般的に強勢を受けないのは、内容語よりも文法的な機能を持つ機能語（冠詞、前置詞、接続詞など）です。以下は太字のところが弱く発音されています。
Ex. 3 l.1-2 **the** process **of** dealing **with the** effects **of** climate change

STEP 3 ▶ 意味を考えながらシャドーイングしましょう。
STEP 4 ▶ 文法や語彙にも注意しながらシャドーイングしましょう。

STEP 3, 4では
できるだけ
文字を見ないで！

☑ Self-Check　How was your shadowing?

😄 Great!	🙂 Good!	😐 Not too bad!	😧 Tough!

≡➤ Fill in the Blanks 🎧 51 Slow 🎧 52 Natural

⑤ Average temperatures in the Middle East (¹   )
(²   ) far faster than* the world's average in the past 30
years. That information comes from the International Monetary
Fund*. And in recent weeks, temperatures in some parts of the
region have reached (³   ) (⁴   ) Celsius.

⑥ Egypt, Morocco and other countries in the region have
been increasing programs for (⁵   ) (⁶   )
(⁷   ), like solar energy.

⑦ Countries meeting at COP27 want to push for* more
international financing to help Middle Eastern countries
(⁸   ) (⁹   ) climate change problems.

⑧ The U.N. has warned that the Middle East's (¹⁰   )
(¹¹   ) could drop 30 percent by 2025. The region is
expected to lose (¹²   ) to (¹³   ) percent of its
GDP* by 2050. The World Bank says the (¹⁴   ) for the
lost economic activity is water scarcity. In Egypt, rain levels
have (¹⁵   ) (¹⁶   ) percent in the past 30 years.

* far faster than
  〜よりはるかに速い
* the International
  Monetary Fund
  (IMF)
  国際通貨基金

* push for
  〜を推し進める

* GDP
  Gross Domestic
  Product
  国内総生産

Main Topics   ⑤〜⑧ の主旨について下記の空欄を埋めましょう。

⑤ Over the past 30 years, average (   ) in the Middle East
  (   ) than the global average.

⑥ (   ) have increased
  their programs for clean energy production.

⑦ The countries participating in COP27 desire (   ) to
  help Middle Eastern countries.

⑧ The U.N. has warned that the Middle East's crop production and its GDP could
  drop due to (   ).

＼＼ Let's Try Shadowing Again! ／／

News 全体または一部のシャドーイングを行いましょう。

✏️ Comprehension

A Answer the questions about problems caused by climate change in the Middle East.

Current Conditions		
1. What has happened in the following countries?	Country ①	
	Country ②	

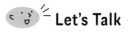

2. What is happening with the temperature in the Middle East?

	In the Future
3. What is expected to happen?	
4. What is the cause of the problems?	

B Vocabulary: Choose the appropriate word. Change the form if necessary.

1. The new factory will provide a lot of employment to the (   ).
2. Keep practicing shadowing every day, and there will be a large (   ) on your pronunciation.
3. (   ) is the total value of all goods and services produced within a country's borders in a specific time period.
4. The government will discuss the (   ) of population decline at the Diet.
5. Last year the country suffered from (   ), leading to water shortages.

> drought / effect / issue / region / GDP

Summary of the News Choose the appropriate word.

The climate problems and financing for climate change will be (1.   ) at this year's COP27. Climate change has (2.   ) the economies of the Middle East. Furthermore, it is predicted that (3.   ) production could decline and GDP could be (4.   ) due to water (5.   ) caused by (6.   ) occurring severe droughts in this area.

> lowered / frequently / damaged / shortages / crop / discussed

😀 **Let's Talk** — Talk about climate change in the Middle East and the actions taken to lessen its impacts.

UN Climate Change Conference to Center on Middle East

Chapter 2

Warm-up

1. Have you heard news reporting the impacts of climate change?

2. Do you feel the effects of climate change on your everyday life?

3. Where do you think people who lost jobs in agriculture move?

Key Words and Phrases   Choose the proper meaning.

- (　) bad social effects
- (　) lose jobs
- (　) climate financing
- (　) developing nations
- (　) mitigation
- (　) changing infrastructure and economies
- (　) rich nations

① 開発途上国
② 社会的悪影響
③ インフラ設備と経済の変化
④ 緩和（温室効果ガス排出の削減）
⑤ 失業する
⑥ 気候変動のための資金提供
⑦ 豊かな国

First Listening   🎧 53 Slow   🎧 54 Natural

まず何も見ないで News の始まり部分を聞きましょう。どれくらい理解できましたか。

About [　　　] %

それでは次のページで文字を見ながらもう一度聞きましょう。

＼＼ **Let's Try Shadowing!** ／／ 🎧 **53** Slow 🎧 **54** Natural

1. The climate damage could also have bad social effects.
2. Karim Elgendy is with Chatham House, a policy group based in* London.

   * based in
   〜を本拠地としている

3. Elgendy said many people in the Middle East who lose jobs in agriculture or tourism will move to cities looking for work. Such changes, Elgendy said, will likely increase unemployment in cities and could raise social problems and affect security.
4. Changing infrastructure and economies to deal with the damage will be costly. The IMF estimates that all these changes will cost 3.3 percent of the region's GDP every year for the next 10 years.
5. The spending has to go toward many needs*. These include better water use systems and new agricultural methods. Other costs include increasing social programs and public information campaigns.

   * has to go toward many needs 多くのニーズのために使わなければならない

STEP 1 内容理解前に、文字を追いながらモデル音声をまねてシャドーイングしましょう。

Main Topics   1 〜 5 の主旨について下記の空欄を埋めましょう。

1. Climate change can have a negative impact on (   ).
2. Karim Elgendy belongs to a (   ).
3. When people who lose their jobs in agriculture and tourism move to (   ), various (   ) could occur.
4. It will be expensive to change (   ) to cope with the damage caused by climate change.
5. The costs will be used for (   ), agricultural methods, and many other things.

内容を理解したら、次の各 **STEP** に注意しながらシャドーイングしましょう。

STEP 2 🄢🄗🄐🄓🄞🄦🄘🄝🄖 🄣🄘🄟🄢 【シャドーイングのラップアップ】

ここまでシャドーイングを練習してだいぶ発話に慣れたことでしょう。同時にリスニング力が付いたと感じているのではないでしょうか。テキストの学習は終わりますが、シャドーイングはこれからも続けてください。テキストで学習したVOA Learning Englishにはインターネットでアクセスできます。

STEP 3 意味を考えながらシャドーイングしましょう。

STEP 4 文法や語彙にも注意しながらシャドーイングしましょう。

> STEP 3, 4 では
> できるだけ
> 文字を見ないで！

☑ **Self-Check**   How was your shadowing?

😄 Great!	🙂 Good!	😐 Not too bad!	😣 Tough!

6 (¹   ) (²   ) (³   ) top issues for developing nations at this year's meeting will be to press* rich nations to provide billions of dollars in promised climate financing.

* press
圧力をかける

7 So far, most of the money provided has gone to helping poorer countries (⁴   ) for reducing greenhouse gas emissions — a process known as "mitigation."

8 Developing nations also want richer countries to show (⁵   ) they will carry out a promise from the last climate meeting to provide $500 billion in financing over the next five years. The idea is to ensure at least (⁶   ) the financing is for adaptation, not mitigation*.

9 However, inflation and a possible* economic recession could make big nations (⁷   ) (⁸   ) (⁹   ).

* for adaptation, not mitigation
単に温室効果ガスの削減策への資金ではなく、将来を見越した対応策を講じるために

* possible
起こりうる

10 International officials often (¹⁰   ) (¹¹   ) to emissions reductions, El Hatow said. She said the countries of Africa, the Middle East and other places in the developing world (¹²   ) (¹³   ) the biggest causes of climate change. But, many of these countries will deal with (¹⁴   ) (¹⁵   ) effects of it.

11 "We need to talk about financing for adaptation," she said, "to adapt to a problem they [developing countries] did not (¹⁶   )."

Main Topics   6 ～ 11 の主旨について下記の空欄を埋めましょう。

6 An important issue at the conference is to have (   ) provide money for dealing with climate change.

7 Most of the money provided so far has been used to reduce (   ).

8 Developing countries want richer countries to show how they will provide (   ) over the next five years.

9 Big countries might not take action quickly due to (   ).

10 Africa, the Middle East, and other developing countries will cope with (   ) of climate change, even though they (   ) the main causes of it.

11 (   ) for dealing with the problem needs to be discussed.

＼＼ Let's Try Shadowing Again! ／／   News 全体または一部のシャドーイングを行いましょう。

▤▷ Comprehension

A Answer the questions and fill in the blank (3).

Climate Change		
Effects	1. Which countries are affected by climate change? (2. What social effects did climate change cause? (	))
Solution	3. Financing is necessary to ( ) the problems. 4. Which countries provide the money? (5. What will the money be used for? Explain more than two things. (	))

B Vocabulary: Choose the appropriate word. Change the form if necessary.
1. (   ) is the basic equipment and structures including transportation systems, buildings, and power supplies.
2. It is probable that (   ) will rise because of the bad economy.
3. More than seventy percent of the land is used for (   ).
4. The company's space project was (   ) by the government.
5. The country announced a goal to reduce carbon dioxide (   ) by 10%.

> agriculture / infrastructure / emissions / finance / unemployment

Summary of the News   Choose the appropriate word.

The people who have lost their jobs (1.   ) to climate change move to (2.   ), which causes many problems. Developing countries are dealing with the (3.   ) problems, although they are not the (4.   ) cause. Therefore, the main (5.   ) of the COP27 is to have richer countries promise to provide this (6.   ).

> climate / due / cost / topic / cities / primary

 **Let's Talk**   Talk about the future social and economic impact of climate change and the costs associated with adapting to climate change.

Japan's New Edible* Cement

\\\ **Let's Try Shadowing!** // 🎧 **57** Slow 🎧 **58** Natural

1. University of Tokyo researchers in Japan have created a new technology that uses food waste in a surprising way.

2. Student Kota Machida and Professor Yuya Sakai say the operation can turn food waste into a strong but bendable* material like cement. They say it is four times stronger than regular concrete, and is sustainable. And, you can eat it, the researchers found.

3. Professor Sakai was looking for a way to replace cement-based concrete with sustainable materials. Cement production releases high levels of carbon dioxide waste into the air, says research group Chatham House.

4. Food waste is a big problem in Japan and the world. In 2019, Japan produced 5.7 million tons of food waste. The government is working on reducing this to 2.7 million by 2030.

5. The food waste that would typically end up in landfills, rotting, and releasing methane gas, can now be used to make the concrete. The material can be reused and buried in the ground if not needed without affecting the environment.

* edible = eatable

* bendable
  曲げることのできる

内容理解前に、文字を追いながらモデル音声をまねてシャドーイングしましょう。

Main Topics 　 ①～⑤ の主旨について下記の空欄を埋めましょう。

① The report is about creation of a new technology to repurpose（　　　　　）at University of Tokyo.

② The repurposed food waste is（　　　　　）than regular concrete and edible.

③ The researcher tried to replace cement-based concrete, which releases large amounts of CO_2, with（　　　　　）materials.

④ Japan's government is attempting to（　　　　　）food waste, a big problem all over the world.

⑤ （　　　　　）now can be used to make the edible concrete without negative effects.

内容を理解したら、次の各 STEP に注意しながらシャドーイングしましょう。

STEP 2　**Shadowing Tips**【英語音の特徴総仕上げ】

▶ 英語のリズム、イントネーション、音声変化などの音声上の特徴が顕著に表れている発話です。発話されているリズム、イントネーション、音がどのように変化しているのかに注意して仕上げのシャドーイングに取り組みましょう。

▶ 話と同時に意味もある程度取り込めるようになりましたね！ Good Job!!!
この記事には、驚く情報が盛り込まれていますよ！

STEP 3　意味を考えながらシャドーイングしましょう。

STEP 3, 4 では
できるだけ
文字を見ないで！

STEP 4　文法や語彙にも注意しながらシャドーイングしましょう。

☑ Self-Check 　How was your shadowing?

😄Great!	🙂Good!	😐Not too bad!	😟Tough!

Appendix 2 ▶ Further Studies

1 We have 17 goals as SDGs, which were adopted at the UN Summit in 2015 by the 193 member countries. See the logos with the notes below and choose the most relevant goal(s) out of 4 goals below.

1) Many people buying clothing are hoping to help the environment by looking to the past. (　　　)

2) The vintage shop does not separate clothes for men and women. (　　　)

3) Vintage shopping is sustainable. (　　　)

1 NO POVERTY

5 GENDER EQUALITY

12 RESPONSIBLE CONSUMPTION AND PRODUCTION

16 PEACE, JUSTICE AND STRONG INSTITUTIONS

(https://www.un.org/sustainabledevelopment/) The content of this publication has not been approved by the United Nations and does not reflect the views of the United Nations or its officials or Member States.

Notes

Goal 1 : End poverty in all its forms everywhere

Goal 5 : Achieve gender equality and empower all women and girls

Goal 12 : Ensure sustainable consumption and production patterns

Goal 16 : Promote just, peaceful and inclusive societies*

*inclusive societies　あらゆる人が参加する社会

2 Fill in the proper word(s) in the blanks based on the chart below.

1) This chart shows the amount of CO_2 emissions per unit (　　　　　).

2) The most sustainable means of passenger transportation out of the four is the (　　　　　).

3) The CO_2 emissions per unit of private car are (　　　　　) double those of a bus.

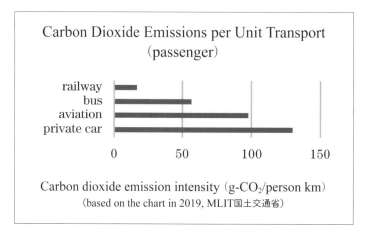

Carbon Dioxide Emissions per Unit Transport (passenger)

Carbon dioxide emission intensity (g-CO_2/person km)
(based on the chart in 2019, MLIT国土交通省)

Appendix 3 ▶ Review of Vocabulary

下記の単語は各 Unit の Comprehension **B** Vocabulary で使われているものです。そこで学習した意味を書き入れましょう。

㊟ v. = verb（動詞）　adj. = adjective（形容詞）　n. = noun（名詞）　prep. = preposition（前置詞）

Unit 1

		品 詞	意 味
1	fuel	v.	
2	impact	v.	
3	produce	v.	
4	serve	v.	
5	switch	v.	

Unit 2

		品 詞	意 味
1	better	v.	
2	critical	adj.	
3	pollute	v.	
4	power	v.	
5	source	n.	

Unit 3

		品 詞	意 味
1	affect	v.	
2	cause	v.	
3	measure	v.	
4	operate	v.	
5	vehicle	n.	

Unit 4

		品 詞	意 味
1	attach	v.	
2	carry out	v.	
3	examine	v.	
4	provide	v.	
5	store	v.	

Unit 5

		品詞	意味
1	appear	v.	
2	change	v.	
3	research	v.	
4	risk	v.	
5	suggest	v.	

Unit 6

		品詞	意味
1	confirm	v.	
2	conservative	adj.	
3	create	v.	
4	frequency	n.	
5	link	n.	

Unit 7

		品詞	意味
1	growth	n.	
2	protect	v.	
3	search	v.	
4	threaten	v.	
5	treat	v.	

Unit 8

		品詞	意味
1	identify	v.	
2	inside	prep.	
3	modern	adj.	
4	ocean	n.	
5	statement	n.	

Unit 9

		品詞	意 味
1	amount	n.	
2	capture	v.	
3	climate	n.	
4	energy	n.	
5	performance	n.	

Unit 10

		品詞	意 味
1	effort	n.	
2	entire	adj.	
3	involve	v.	
4	reduce	v.	
5	transportation	n.	

Unit 11

		品詞	意 味
1	brand	v.	
2	combine	v.	
3	price	v.	
4	save	v.	
5	waste	n.	

Unit 12

		品詞	意 味
1	carry	v.	
2	goal	n.	
3	period	n.	
4	promise	v.	
5	separate	v.	

Unit 13

		品 詞	意 味
1	drought	n.	
2	effect	n.	
3	GDP	n.	
4	issue	n.	
5	region	n.	

Unit 14

		品 詞	意 味
1	agriculture	n.	
2	emission	n.	
3	finance	v.	
4	infrastructure	n.	
5	unemployment	n.	

編著者

倉本 充子（くらもと　あつこ）

西田 晴美（にしだ　はるみ）

釣井 千恵（つりい　ちえ）

John Nevara（ジョン・ネバラ）

シャドーイングでスキルアップ

― VOA Learning English でいまを読む―

2024年2月20日　第1版発行

編著者── 倉本充子・西田晴美・釣井千恵・John Nevara
発行者── 前田俊秀
発行所── 株式会社　三修社
　　　　　〒150-0001　東京都渋谷区神宮前 2-2-22
　　　　　TEL 03-3405-4511
　　　　　FAX 03-3405-4522
　　　　　振替 00190-9-72758
　　　　　https://www.sanshusha.co.jp
　　　　　編集担当　三井るり子
印刷所── 日経印刷株式会社

©2024 Printed in Japan　ISBN978-4-384-33531-6 C1082

表紙デザイン　　　　　峯岸孝之
本文デザイン・DTP　　大貫としみ（ME TIME）
準拠音声制作　　　　　高速録音株式会社

教科書準拠CD発売

本書の準拠CDをご希望の方は弊社までお問い合わせください。